From

The Women's Press Ltd
34 Great Sutton Street, London EC1V 0DX

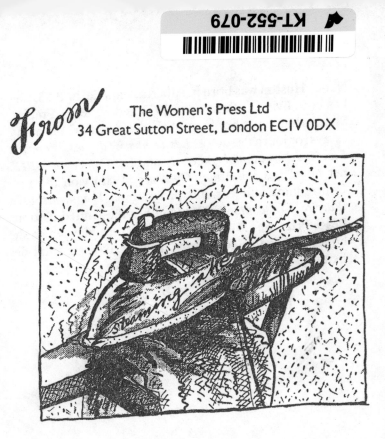

Nancy Huston was born in Alberta, Canada, in 1953. She has been living in Paris since 1973 and writes in French. She has had seven books published and has written many essays for journals such as *Les Temps Modernes*, *Women's Studies International Quarterly* and *Les Cahiers du GRIF*. her novel *Les Variations Goldberg* (1981) won the Prix Contrepoint and a radio programme *Fragments of a Warrior's Discourse* (1981) won her the United Nations Peace Prize. She is currently working on a play which she hopes to have staged by the Théâtre Experimental des Femmes in Montreal.

NANCY HUSTON

The Story of Omaya

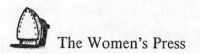

The Women's Press

First published in this translation by
The Women's Press Limited 1987
A Member of the Namara Group
34 Great Sutton Street, London EC1V 0DX

First published as *Histoire d'Omaya* by Éditions du Seuil 1985

Copyright © Éditions du Seuil 1985
This translation copyright © Nancy Huston 1987

British Library Cataloguing in Publication Data
Huston, Nancy
    The story of Omaya.
    I. Title   II. Histoire d' Omaya. *English*
    843'.914[F]   PQ2668.U8/

    ISBN 0-7043-5021-1
    ISBN 0-7043-4049-6 Pbk

Typeset by AKM Associates (UK) Ltd,
Ajmal House, Hayes Road, Southall, Greater London
Printed and bound in Great Britain by
Hazell Watson & Viney Ltd,
Aylesbury, Bucks

Dedication

What can I add?

That in order to write this book I could only oscillate between two choices, either madly projecting myself onto you through the use of 'I', or madly distancing myself from you through the use of 'she'. And yet I never forgot that *you* exist. Truly. Outside the book. Nor that your story actually took place. I hope that in fashioning this character, whose story is partly like yours and partly like my own – but who by that very token is neither you nor I – I have not betrayed us.

The truth I have tried to tell is the one I saw on your face, one winter's day, in a court of law. That face has a name, that day has a date, that court has a location. But the truth went so very far beyond these facts that I could only tell it by silencing them. Thus, the book is dedicated to *you* – and also to every other woman who, deafened by the clamour of facts, has experienced the same truth in silence.

Stuck. It's got stuck again and Omaya is struggling with it. I've spent my whole life struggling with zips, it seems I've never done anything but that, try to insert the little piece of metal into the hole, it goes in but then gets stuck, and I can't pull up the tongue, my fingers are gigantic and numb, Omaya sees every wrinkle on every knuckle, deep ridges in the dry flesh, nibbled skin around the fingernails, white spots underneath, Omaya's fingers try to make the zip slide but it's broken, I'm absolutely sure, it won't ever work again and I'm freezing cold, the fingers grow impatient, shake the tongue, yank at it violently, it gets stuck, and now, beneath the thick forest fringe, my pores begin to exude a viscous liquid, the others can't see it but they find me laughable just the same, I've been fiddling with this tongue for the past ten minutes and still haven't got the better of it . . . Other people dress without thinking, their hands performing nimble gestures without their brain having to get involved, other people dress and undress in arabesques, objects don't resist anyone but Omaya, it has to close sooner or later, I refuse to acknowledge defeat, they all hope I'm going to collapse the way I did the last time, but today I won't give them that satisfaction, I won't even raise my eyes, I'll answer all their questions in a neutral,

1

objective tone of voice, and they won't get the better of me. The same questions, the same answers. It's like a role. All I have to do is play it as professionally as possible, Anastasia swore that this time it would work, virtually swore, that if I behaved congenially, if I made an effort, if I concentrated on making a good impression upon the audience, letting them see my real smile instead of my snarl . . .

When Granny made an effort, for example to open a jar of crab-apple jelly, her grimace was impossible to distinguish from a smile. Often, having smiled back at her, I'd be disconcerted to see her mouth relax suddenly and her lips go slack: the lid had finally yielded. Now – the spitting image of her mother, one thing leading to another – it's Cybele who grimaces like that. Bent over her computations, her head supported by her left hand, her hair falling over wrist, arm and shoulder, her face is distorted by the same false smile. After the death of Cybele it will be my turn. Or perhaps already, right now, with the zip . . . is Omaya smiling at this very moment? A true smile or a false one? Does the audience think she's having fun? Stop it, they're not even looking at her, they're sleeping, they're reading, they're talking to each other – they're talking about me – no, they're not talking about Omaya, this mustn't start up again, especially not now, stop it! Omaya should concentrate, she should pay attention to what she's doing. But my fingers! My fingers are dried and chapped from the cold, yellowed by tobacco . . . Omaya mustn't look at her fingers, only at the zip. That, too, is a smile, a sardonic grin, two rows of metallic teeth sneering at me, two long black lips parted in a nasty, sniggering laugh . . .

2

'Keep your mouth open, I'm warning you . . . If you bite us, you'll be sorry.'

It's got to close, oh my God oh my God I want to *close* it. I do know how zips work, first you insert the little piece of metal into the hole, all the way in, that's right, and then you hold the bottom of the zip between your thumb and index finger, don't move, then you pull on the metal tongue with the other hand . . . There, it's coming, it's finally coming, oh my God I've done it, the mouth has closed at last, the mouth has swallowed up Omaya. Omaya is nice and warm, she's going to calm down now, she lays her hands on her knees, she looks at neither hands nor zip, she shuts her eyes, she can go to sleep, she doesn't have to pay attention to the stops because she won't get off till the very last one, someone will wake her up, everybody off, she'll have arrived and everything will go just fine . . .

But Omaya can't sleep any more. She has to stay on guard. Vigilant. One never knows. It can happen anywhere, any time. One must be careful . . . *Alert! Alarm! Achtung!*

'Sorry.'

He touched my foot, he ran into me, over me . . . *Achtung!* No . . . He did touch Omaya's foot, that's true, but he didn't do it on purpose, he said he was sorry, they said they regretted what had happened, withdraw your complaint, I beg you, you won't accomplish anything this way, all you'll do is make yourself even more miserable and ill, if you persist. And in any case, are you quite certain of the identity? Are you sure you've got the right man? No, you see, it can't be him. He never takes the underground, he never goes anywhere except by car. It definitely isn't him. And what about your own identity?

3

Are you certain of it? Are you really the same woman as the one whose December experiences you've described? This *is* the month of December, but is it the *same* month of December? Always the same words . . .

There was that song, it was about loneliness and living in a womb, about touching and being touched by no one, about hiding, taking refuge from the winter, in the depth and in the darkness of December . . .

Every time I heard that song, it would be the month of December. It's always been the month of December. I've spent my whole life listening to that song and thinking: Ah! It's December again. Omaya is freezing. The mouth has closed, she's huddled up inside, she never wants to come out again, it's too cold, how am I ever going to speak to them? Answer the same questions all over again. Relive the month of December all over again. When she plays a role, Omaya knows how to get into the skin of the character and bring it to life. When she has to speak in her own name, it doesn't work. She mumbles her lines, the words coagulate on her tongue – how can anyone be expected to believe her? Do you swear to tell the truth, the whole truth, and nothing but the truth? Raise your right hand and say: I swear. Lower your hand. And what about your smiles – are they true or false? And your tears? Mightn't they be the tears of an actress? And your testimony – how can we be sure? Try to control yourself, young lady. The interrogation cannot proceed under these conditions.

'What time did you leave the Castle?'
'. . . I'm sorry, could you repeat the question?'
'What time did you get home last night?'
'Get home?'

4

'Yes, get home. You weren't in bed at one in the morning. I looked.'

'. . .'

'You'd climbed out the window?'

'. . . Yes.'

'In your nightdress?'

'Yes.'

'And then?'

'I went to Alix's.'

'You'd arranged to meet her?'

'Yes.'

'What next? What did you do? Don't make me play guessing games, I'll lose my patience. What did you do?'

'Nothing, we just talked, that's all.'

'Where did you talk?'

'Sitting on the kerb in front of her house. We looked at the stars.'

'You're lying. I called Alix's place, her mother searched everywhere for you, you'd gone roaming the streets, isn't that right?'

'Yes, that's right.'

'In your nightdress.'

'Yes.'

'You were out walking round the streets in the middle of the night, half naked – you dare to tell me that's what you were doing?'

'It was such a mild night, we felt like going for a stroll.'

'Where did you go?'

'We just went up and down in front of the house, that's all.'

'Don't tell me that's all, I know when you say that's all you must be lying. I can't stand being lied to – do you hear me?'

'Yes.'

'Where did you go?'

'We went . . .'

'Stop trying to think something up. Tell me the truth. Look me in the eye. Tell me the truth.'

'We went . . .'

'Don't start blubbering, it won't get you anywhere. Well?'

'. . . to the coffee-shop on the corner.'

'To the coffee-shop! In your nightdress?'

'. . . Yes.'

'You must be out of your mind!'

She's completely out of her mind! That's not the way it happened at all!

Omaya is not out of her mind, she has nothing to fear, all she has to do is remain calm and everything will be all right, Cybele will come. She loves me. She's always said so: It's not you I hate, it's your lies, do you understand? *You* I love, but I detest your lying to me. Go to sleep now, my little one. Cybele is here. Cybele is not here. She's never here. But she will come. Always in the future. She will love me. As long as I tell the truth. The truth does exist, Omaya, whatever you may think. Clarity is synonymous with beauty. Why do you insist on making things obscure?

You're the one who hid your eyes, Cybele. Concerning the Owl. You're the one who absolutely insisted on remaining in the dark. That time, you let the sunlight of truth shine just for me. Blazing, incandescent. Not that it's of the least importance now, of course. The Owl won't come, he can't do any more harm. From him I inherited the vacant eyes, and from you the false smile.

6

The razor-blade starts slashing: first Omaya's fingers, then her wrists, her throat, her lips, her eyes. It cuts at her with clean, swift strokes, digging a valley into her flesh, the valley fills up with dark red water but it doesn't overflow. It all happens in a flash, in silence. Especially the eyes. Slicing the eyeballs, over and over. They are two grapes so ripe that the skin has split and a deep crevice runs from one end to the other. Here – take these new eyes, nice glass ones, two marbles. They'll help you to see clearly. Put them in . . . No, not in your mouth! Omaya chews and the glass is pulverised by her teeth. She swallows and the slivers of glass shred her throat as they go down. There are rivulets of blood, but there is no pain.

The owl had eyes of glass, yellow marbles with dark circles at the centre, I never looked at them close up but I know that's what they were like, even today I can see them, they're far more real than the eyes of the man who bumped into me a moment ago and is scrutinising me now. It was at Granny's house, the owl was perched on the mantelpiece in the den right next to my bedroom, and if the door was open I couldn't pass in front of it to go downstairs, I would have awakened the owl who slept with its eyes wide open, I would have heard a ruffling of feathers, its head would have pivoted towards me and its yellow eyes would have caught sight of me, ferocious golden marbles beneath two feather-bristling brows, its wings would have started beating and its hooked beak clicking, the owl would have flown across the room and swooped down on me and I would have been dead. Of course, it was the owl that was dead, Omaya knows that very well, even at the time she knew it, it was dead but only on condition that the door to the den remained closed. If it were left open, one had to expect the worst.

'Cybele! Come upstairs!'

'What do you want?'

'Come and close the door to the den!'

'Oh, darling, you're not going to make the same scene every year, are you? Come on down and have your breakfast.'

'I can't!'

'Okay, stay in bed, have a good day!'

'Mother, PLEASE!'

Silence. Omaya gets back into bed. She cries until her eyelids have swollen sufficiently to cover her pupils. Then, blinded, she runs the length of the hall and throws herself at the staircase . . .

The man sitting across from me is staring at me. His feet are all I can see of him, but he can see the whole of Omaya. He's looking her over, his eyes are travelling up and down her body, up and down. Between his boots: a long, flattened, dusty cigarette-end. Decipher the brand name upside-down. He wants to force me to raise my eyes, he wants to pierce my defenceless pupils and get into my brain, from there go down through my body, making my heart thump, my nipples stiffen, my hands tremble. He wants to make me melt beneath his fiery gaze, a stroke of lightning that would turn me into a quivering mass of jelly. Omaya is not afraid. Omaya can confront his gaze and return it. Omaya's eyes are not a window but a mirror. A mirror of ice. Light cannot penetrate them, it is reflected off them. Omaya raises her eyes, accepts the challenge. The man is asleep, his head slumped to one side, his mouth agape, his lower lip hanging down. He has hair in his nostrils, black wiry hair on his chin and cheeks, tufts of hair in the hollow of his neck between the breastbone and the Adam's apple, hair on his fingers, on

8

the backs of his folded hands, on his wrists. Hairs sprout up around a wedding-ring on the left hand and around a wristwatch on the right, they're stuck in the links of the watchband, I'm going to be sick.

Omaya gets to her feet, she needs air, all the air in the car is streaked with long black hairs, they sweep across the space like vines, twining themselves into a net that grows tighter and more suffocating by the second ... Panting ... Mustn't panic ... *Achtung*! No – it's her own fringe, it's just Omaya's fringe that she wears so long, always too long, so that it falls over her eyes like a curtain. Peek through the curtains to see whether the house is full. Will there be a big audience tonight? Squint hard to try and make out, beyond the footlights, the bodies of the judges seated in the dark.

'Don't you want to have a parting and hold your hair back with slides? Or else wear it behind your ears?'

'No. I like my fringe the way it is.'

'Well, then, I'll have to cut it. It's really much too long. You're going to ruin your eye-sight, you can't see a thing.'

'Yes, I can. I can see just fine. I can see everything I want to see.'

'You can't see a thing, you're always squinting. If you go on like this you'll have wrinkles before you reach puberty. Come and sit down.'

'I don't want to.'

'Come on, darling. No wonder you've got so clumsy lately. You're always running into furniture and knocking your glass over at meals, it's because of your fringe. You have such a pretty face, why not show it to other people? Come on.'

The scissors glinting under the kitchen bulb. Gigantic, dazzling blades.

'Shut your eyes.'

Omaya keeps her eyes open. The curtain goes up.

'Now, look at yourself in the mirror.'

Wan, childish face, a portion of forehead bared and whiter than the rest.

'It isn't straight, I've cut it crooked, the left side is shorter than the right. Come back.'

Blades in front of open eyes.

'Now take a look.'

Moonlike monkey-face.

'Oh, no! Now the right side is shorter than the left! One more try and then I'll stop.'

'I don't want to.'

'Oh, darling, we can't leave it like that! You know what you look like? A little clown. Come on, sit down, I promise this will be the last time.'

The blades hack at the eyes, reducing them to mush. The scissors are metamorphosed into a double-bladed axe. Cybele holds the axe next to my forehead, she gives two or three small preliminary taps – like before cutting into a fresh, tough-barked log – and then, with a single clean stroke, she removes the top of my skull. She proceeds downwards slice by slice; the whole of my head is removed only after the fourth stroke. Cybele contemplates the result with satisfaction. Her expression resembles that of a surgeon after the success of a delicate operation.

'You should be ashamed to make such a fuss about a little haircut. You hair isn't part of you, you know, it's just dead cells. Your nails too. It doesn't hurt at all to cut them. You don't know what real pain is. I can tell you that when I gave birth to you . . .'

'Yes, I know. They opened your stomach. They cut you.'

'They certainly did. Cut into the living flesh.'

'And . . . did you see it? With your own eyes?'

'Of course not. I was under anaesthetic.'

'What about the Owl? Did he see it? Was he there?'

'No, darling, there are things that even owls can't see. There were only doctors and nurses – at least I assume so, I don't know for sure, I wasn't conscious.'

'If you weren't conscious, you couldn't feel it when they cut you?'

'No. Pain before, pain afterwards. And in the middle: Omaya.'

Omaya in the middle of the wound. She is freezing. The valley fills up with dark red water but it doesn't overflow. There is no pain. The Owl, he who sees all, sees nothing. Excluded from the scarlet stage.

'And afterwards?'

'I've already told you. You were so weak they had to put you in a glass box. You lived in a room with the other babies in boxes. There was a huge window with a velvet curtain. When we came to see you, your father and I, we never knew whether the curtain would be open or closed . . .'

Peek through the curtains, screw up your eyes: who's out there? Who has the right to look at Omaya?

The curtain goes up. Everything is determined in advance – music, costumes, make-up, props, phrases rehearsed a thousand times, invariable choreography, gestures perfected in front of the mirror – this is the framework of my freedom. Everything is artificial – the feelings, the words, the motives – this is the framework of my truth. Omaya borrows someone else's voice, and that is what allows her to exist. She borrows someone else's body, someone else's

11

memories, someone else's tastes and distastes, and that is what makes her real. She says words of love to men she doesn't love, she laughs at lines that aren't amusing, she grows indignant on command and feels genuine anger rising within her, anger which is unspoken and unspeakable offstage. She shrieks, implores, tears out her hair, and no one holds it against her. On the contrary, they applaud. Omaya writhes on the floor; they applaud. Omaya chants lewd verses; they applaud. Omaya is happy.

Never has she forgotten a line, virtually never: onstage, words flow naturally from her mouth. She takes her script, goes off into the forest, and walks along a path reading aloud to herself, the rhythms of the text respond to the rhythms of her body, the mingling of legs, heart, lungs and words seems to her divinely obvious: it has to be those particular words and no others, Omaya reads aloud and the bronchi hold their breath, the trees exhort her: Go on! Omaya begins again, this time she presses the script to her chest and walks faster and talks faster, the script is already imprinted on her memory, its syllables already meshed with her organs. When the show is over, these words will vanish into thin air. The deck will be cleared. The page will be blank. Not a trace. The sets will be dismantled, the costumes put away, the memories of the character effaced, and the whole thing can start again. Always from zero.

As long as Omaya is someone else, she knows what she has to say; it's in real life that her lines desert her. She stands before her judges – only this time they are no longer seated in the dark, they are on stage, and they demand that she prove her innocence.

'Why did you leave the Castle?'

'Excuse me . . . Could you repeat the question?'
'Why did you leave University?'

Omaya has an exam to write, she's late, she rushes out of the house and plunges into the bowels of the earth, the train arrives, she gets on but at the next station notices it's going the wrong direction, she gets off again, her heart pounding, and jumps onto an escalator . . . At the top, corridors extend as far as the eye can see, their walls are splashed with naked women, she runs down one corridor after another, dragging behind her a heavy bag filled with the books she needs for the exam . . . Frantic, she arrives at last at the university campus, follows red arrows on concrete columns, Examination Room, Examination Room, the hour is long past, will they even let her in? . . . When she gets to the lecture theatre, she discovers thousands of students all bent over at the same angle, noses grazing booklets, she makes her way down a narrow aisle between two rows of desks, on the front platform an invigilator greets her curtly, hands over the blank pages she is required to fill, the subject is printed at the top in capital letters that leap out at her face: THE CHALLENGE OF EDUCATION. Oh, no! I've come to the wrong room, I can't write about that, I'm terribly sorry, it wasn't this exam I was supposed to write but a different one, I have nothing to say on that subject, let me go, I beg of you, let me go!

Omaya goes up the six steps to the school holding Cybele by the hand. It's a Saturday afternoon. Cybele lets go of Omaya to shake the hand of a man with a moustache. Then she's in her car, her hand is blowing me a kiss – but she's the one who made this appointment – and she's gone.

13

The man with the moustache leads the little girl into his office and sits her down in an armchair. He takes a seat across from her, behind a vast table covered with papers and books. We spend the whole afternoon playing games: Omaya manipulates cubes, cylinders and pyramids of different colours and shapes, she folds and unfolds pieces of paper, she answers every question put to her by the man's soft, warm voice. At the same time, she's aware that the point is not to play games but to prove something, yet she can't work out exactly what is at stake, as the hours go by she grows more and more nervous, she likes the man with the moustache and she's afraid of disappointing him . . . Towards evening, handing Omaya a glass of orange juice, the man tells her to say words. Any words at all, words at random, anything that comes into her head.

Omaya feels her mind gradually emptying, as though she were swallowing, along with the orange juice, all the language she'd ever learned, swallowing her tongue. She barely manages to salvage a few nouns: table . . . chair . . . wall . . . paper . . . book . . . office . . . school . . . city . . . country . . . tree . . . forest . . . road . . . car . . . She hesitates, there's nothing left, her mind is a blank. If she looks around her, the man will notice that she's already run out of ideas and is using the objects in front of her for inspiration . . . Forcing herself to keep her eyes on the floor while she records the contents of the room, she proceeds with difficulty: desk . . . paper . . . no, I've already said paper, I'm not supposed to say the same word twice . . . man . . . woman . . . boy . . . girl . . . baby . . . photograph . . . postcard . . . letter . . . pen . . . table . . . chair . . . this is awful, he must think I'm ridiculous, I've already said table and chair . . . er, music . . . charming . . . chair . . . er . . . table . . . Her voice stops. Silence. Is that all? says the man. She nods her head, annihilated.

14

When she wakes up, the man is standing above her, behind her armchair, leaning over . . . That's all. It stops there.

'It stops there?'
'You mean that still isn't enough?'
'It stops there, or your mind goes blank?'

Cybele never runs out of ideas. She spends her time sitting in front of the computer that takes up a whole wall of her office. She doesn't know how beautiful she is, her hair piled on top of her head, her thighs parted slightly on the stool. I watch her and she watches the screen full of dancing figures and letters, the submissive subjects of her long, tapered fingers that fly across the keys at the speed of light. All around the screen there are red and green and blue lights twinkling, if I looked at them through my eyelashes they might resemble a Christmas tree, but Cybele has always despised that sort of nonsense, she's measuring intelligence. It's a delicate and difficult job, she's been at it for months and years, she travels from country to country, attending conferences, keeping up with all the breakthroughs, all the latest progress in her field, giving lectures, brilliant, scintillating speeches, slicing through flak, the scissors under the lightbulb, she invents new and improved programmes, new and improved questionnaires, new and improved intelligence tests, she splits open the Owl's head with her axe and a little girl springs forth, she splits open people's heads with her axe to see what's inside, artificial intelligence, electronic brains, differentiation of cerebral functions, fast circuits, slow circuits, short circuits. Cybele smiles at the computer screen – but it's her false smile, the grimace of effort – and the computer responds with knowing winks of its numberless eyes.

'Your father used to be a very intelligent man, you know.'

'Is that why you married him?'

'Oh . . . Does anyone know why they marry someone? What I do know is that I was curious to see what a child of his and mine would be like. What the crossing of that genetic patrimony and matrimony would result in.'

'And . . . are you satisfied with the result?'

'What a question! You know I adore you. Even if I do sometimes think you're wasting that precious heritage by doing drama. But that's your decision, isn't it?'

'Yes, that's my decision.'

The man with the black hairs has disappeared. Behind Omaya, above her, another man. He just stands there. I can't see him but I can sense him very strongly. He doesn't move, he knows that I know he's there, that I'm only pretending to be unaware of him, his gaze slithers into the half-open mouth of my jacket. Guess what's underneath. And underneath the underneath. And so on: strip off the jacket, the jersey, the blouse, the underwear, the skin. Peel away the strips of skin. The flayed virgins. They'd make a superficial incision and then peel the woman from head to foot like an orange. A priest would don the virgin's skin to absorb her fertility and her strength. He'd walk through the village dressed like that, bringing prosperity for the year to come. The virgin would be lying at the edge of the road, dust sticking to her raw flesh. The yellow dogs would chew at her, fattening themselves on her fat.

Omaya yanks at the zip of her jacket. The mouth closes around her neck. She turns around, no one is there.

'Why do you keep turning round?'

. . .

'Are you afraid there might be another exit to my office, a secret door through which I might escape?'

'The Lords have the keys to all the secret doors.'

'What Lords?'

. . .

'I assure you that this office has only one door.'

He's there, above me, behind me, Omaya's words coagulate on her lips, the air can't get through, I shouldn't be lying on my back, I can't breathe, I should be sitting up in an armchair . . .

For example: Omaya is sitting on the toilet in the ladies' room, in the basement of a restaurant. And then, all of a sudden, a man is staring at her from above. She's unable to raise her eyes, unable to get to her feet, she's pinned down. Nailed to the spot. The man says nothing, he does nothing, he just looks at her from above, his presence fills Omaya's throat and nostrils, asphyxiating her. Panting. Night after night, she struggles to catch her breath.

Cybele and the Owl had taken me out to eat in a restaurant, it was to celebrate Cybele's *viva* exam, we were very gay. Tiny girl proud of being grown up, I wend my way through the legs of people and chairs and tables, all the way to the back, all the way down a dark hall next to the noisy kitchen, next to the swinging doors of the kitchen, all the way to the toilet and I stand on tiptoes to lock the door. Pants down I hoist myself onto the seat, pants up I flush the toilet, the water starts to swirl and rise up higher and higher, it will never go back down, it's going to overflow and flood the hermetically sealed room and keep on rising, eddying about my ankles, my waist,

17

my head, no one will hear the screams of a little girl over the clanging pots and pans, the shouted orders of the waiters, my parents are at the far end of the restaurant, so far away, I'll never see them again. Hammering on the door. Tearing the skin off my fingers clawing at the lock. And afterwards, having to bear the condescending smiles of the authentically grown-up grown-ups.

The water goes round and round, it's a vortex. If you stir a spoon in a cup of coffee or a bowl of soup, it will create spirals. If you hold the spoon vertically and release it, it will go through the surface of the liquid and plunge to the bottom. If you hold the spoon horizontally and lay it down gently, it will remain there, a tiny empty miracle: the surface of the liquid will hold it up. There is tension between molecules, they adhere strongly to one another, they coagulate. If you pour water, drop by drop, into a glass that's already full, it can go higher than the top of the glass without spilling. The surface of the water will be taut and curved like a full belly. Another drop, yet another, the glass is more than full but it doesn't overflow. If you throw a stone into the lake, concentric circles will appear on the surface of the water. If you break the ice on the surface of the lake, bubbles will appear: at first elliptic, elongated, irregular as amoebas, and then, scarcely a second later, circular. Everything tends towards round-ness, towards the perfection of the circle. If Omaya stretches out on the water and relaxes, the surface will hold her up. She can give herself up to the infinite arms of the lake.

The Owl's the one who taught her all these things. She's forgotten the explanations: weight, mass, gravity, centri-fugal and centripetal force. She can remember nothing but her amazement: the spoon is floating! Omaya is floating! The bubbles are round! So are the earth and the sun!

The water of the lake is motionless. This is December and the water is frozen, it doesn't move, and the circles are being made by the Owl. He goes around the lake, hands clasped behind his back, chin on chest, shoulders bent forward. He's a hunchback. As the earth rotates around the sun, so the Owl rotates around the lake. Why, Daddy? He'll never explain anything to me again. If I approach him, he'll raise his vacant eyes to look at me. He won't recognise me. He'll mutter a few ancient, dismembered phrases under his breath, let out an indignant exclamation or a piercing laugh, and then resume his circular march.

He won't come.

'You mustn't disturb your father.'

'Is he ill?'

'No, he's working, he needs peace and quiet so he can concentrate.'

'He won't be having supper with us?'

'No, he told me he wanted to work all evening. He won't come out until the middle of the night. Like an owl.'

'Can't I say goodnight to him before I go to bed?'

'It's better not to . . . You'll see, he'll come back to us before long. But for a while we'll have to humour him. Not make any noise when we go past his door.'

'Walk on tiptoes?'

'That's right. We'll be like two little mice. We're very, very frightened of the big old owl. He mustn't hear us.'

'Or else he'll swoop down on us . . .'

'And eat us! . . . Okay, shall we have some supper?'

Omaya isn't hungry. The earth is round as an orange. Peel the orange and flatten out the peel to make a map. Peel the skin upwards from the rump until it covers the face. The dogs chew at the virgin.

'We're not going to eat you! Are you out of your mind? All we want to do is have a little fun. What's the matter, don't you like men? You prefer women? Stop squirming. Hold still. Hold her down, will you? Jesus Christ . . .'

'You're not hungry?'
'No.'
'You don't want anything to eat?'
'No.'
'Not even an orange?'
'No, thank you.'
'A bit of liver, the heart that's ceased to beat?'

Omaya walks home as fast as she can, she's having guests over tonight, Alix will be there along with three or four Friends to help her start her new life in the Flat. Cradled in her arms like a baby is the chicken she has just bought at the market. She forgot to ask them to clean it for her. She carried it off just as it was, wrapped in plain white paper to hide the cold pink flesh, the head with its narrow eye-slits, the claws curling as if to retrieve something which had escaped their clutch. In the kitchen of the Flat, on the table, Omaya spreads open the paper around the chicken. Silence. The chicken doesn't move. Knife. The chicken is an animal. The neck is its neck. The drumsticks are its thighs. Spread apart the thighs. Slip the knife in between the bones, at the joint. Saw. The wings are its wings. And inside, it's unspeakable. Omaya vomits. When the Friends arrive, her hands are still bloody and her face haggard. Impossible to serve them anything.

Omaya chokes. Chicken neck stuffed down her throat. Blue-veined skin sliding on the muscle, wrinkling back and forth. A neck inside her neck. She wants to vomit but she's pinned down. OPEN THROAT SHALL BE LAW.

'What time did they let you go? They say they dropped you off at eleven o'clock, whereas you claim . . .'

'Objection, your Honour. The use of the verb "to say" for the accused and "to claim" for my client is inadmissible.'

'Did you have a nice New Year's Eve? What time did you get home?'

'I get home whenever I want now, Cybele.'

'Yes, of course . . . It's just that I called you last night and a strange voice answered. I never know who's going to pick up the phone at your place. How many of you are there living in the flat these days?'

'I live with whoever I want now, Cybele.'

'You don't have to be so hostile. Why do you speak to me in that tone of voice? Don't I have the right to take an interest in what you're doing any more?'

'You're not interested. You just want to know for the sake of knowing, so that nothing I do can escape you. Come over for a drink tomorrow and I'll tell you about my New Year's Eve in person.'

'You know I can't just jump onto an aeroplane in the middle of the conference. Even if I really do want to see you. Please don't be sarcastic, Omaya . . . What's the matter?'

'Excuse me, but I have a hard time communicating through these modern gadgets. I'm not a woman of my

21

century, I suppose. I still prefer human beings to machines.'

'Okay. Listen, I can tell you don't feel like talking to me today, so I'll leave you alone. Are you in good health, at least? Are you eating well?'

'I'm eating, drinking, smoking, fucking – just fine, thanks.'

Cybele hangs up. She must be dissolving into tears a little bit, way over there, but emotion is hard to sustain when its source is separated from you by several oceans and several continents. She is day and I am night.

I'm eating, that's a lie. Omaya is wonderfully light these days. Especially her head. So light it sometimes starts to vibrate softly, humming like a motor. Her hands and feet tingle. Her nerves become electric wires. Omaya is devoid of flesh. Pure intelligence. Artificial and cold. She trembles with cold.

'At least try and eat a little bit, Miss. You haven't even touched your tray.'

'I told you I was incapable of swallowing anything. You shouldn't have bothered to bring me a tray.'

'But you've got to eat something! You're going to disappear if you go on fasting like this.'

'Leave me alone. How many times –'

'Don't get excited!'

'Don't get excited, young lady. You have nothing to fear within the confines of the court.'

'Don't get excited, I'm warning you. Stop screaming or we'll give you a good reason to scream. Stop it, do you hear? Fuck . . .'

Omaya hears the women's screams. She's so cold, she's freezing cold, she ties the electric wires of her body into knots beneath the blankets, she hears the women shouting obscenities, insulting their parents, their lovers, their husbands, their children and God; syllables spew from their throats like vomit, they've swallowed their tongues, half digested them and now they're spitting up words at random, verbal gobs . . .

'DON'T TOUCH ME!'
'Don't get excited, I told you.'

I'm cold, I'll be cold for ever.

'Get in, you must be cold.'
'Thank you for stopping.'
'Aren't you afraid of hitch-hiking around all by yourself?'
'No, why? Should I be afraid?'
'You hear a lot of crazy things . . .'
'Yes, but I always get picked up by men like you, who've heard a lot of crazy things and want to keep them from happening to me.'
'Oh! That's good . . . How are you doing – a bit warmer now?'
'Just fine, thanks.'

Spread apart the thighs. Slip the knife in between the bones, at the joint. Twist the neck. Cut off the head, with a single clean stroke of the double-bladed axe. Madly in love. I don't want to be flesh. I'm so çold. Goose-flesh. Disarticulated. Dismembered. Destroyed.

'Hello!'

'Oh, hello! I didn't see you.'

'Nor did I . . . How have you been?'

'Oh, fine. What about you?'

'Fine, I suppose. As well as can be expected.'

'I know what you mean . . . Cold weather we're having, isn't it?'

'I'll say it is! Even at the office we freeze to death.'

'So do we. It's because the government doesn't want to fork out any money for new radiators. They say it isn't worth it, since we're going to be moving soon anyway . . .'

'Yes, but when? They've been talking about moving for years, and we're still in the same old building, freezing to death. My hands are so cold I make typing errors.'

'Does your boss hold it against you?'

'Oh, no, it doesn't matter to him, as long as I correct them. Sometimes he hands the letters back and I have to retype them.'

'Ah yes . . .'

'That way it takes me twice as long to do the same amount of work. Sometimes it's past six by the time I leave.'

'That does make a long day, doesn't it?'

'Are you going away for the holidays?'

'No, I've already taken six days off in September, when my son was ill. If I take more now, there won't be anything left for the summer.'

'What was the matter with your son?'

'Oh, an ear infection. At the day-care centre there's no way to avoid it. The children just keep passing their illnesses back and forth.'

'Oh – he's just a baby, then?'

'Yes, twenty-seven months . . . What about you – do you have children?'

'I have a daughter but she's much older – almost ten.'

24

'Oh, yes, that is different. They grow fast, don't they?'

'They certainly do! It's dreadful . . .'

'I bought my son a pair of winter boots in October, and they're already too small. And children's shoes are scandalously expensive.'

'I know, it's outrageous. My daughter is hypersensitive about clothes – whenever a girl in her class shows up wearing something new, she wants to have the same. I tell her no – in the first place, I can't afford it, and in the second place, she doesn't really need it.'

'You're absolutely right . . . What about you – will you be going away for the holidays?'

'Oh, we go skiing. Same place every year. My husband's the one that really insists on it, but then the little one enjoys taking lessons . . . and it does make for a change of scene.'

'Ah, yes, it's important to have a change of scene from time to time, isn't it? Otherwise . . .'

'See that young woman over there?'

'The blonde?'

'Yes.'

'She looks like . . . fallen out of bed.'

'Doesn't she just? She might at least have brushed her hair before she left the house.'

'Her trousers look like they've been slept in.'

'For a month!'

'What a nerve to appear in public looking like that!'

'She's much too young to be a tramp.'

'Other people have to look at her – she could show a bit of respect.'

'Self-respect, if nothing else.'

'It's perfectly shameful.'

'I must interrupt. In your first statement, you spoke of

25

your client's so called forest fringe as being made up of *black* hairs, not *blonde* ones.'

'If I'd described the hair of the man sitting across from her as being blonde, no one would have believed that Omaya could have found him disturbing.'

'You are requested to stick strictly to the facts. This kind of prevarication is inadmissible. Clerk, please take note that this young woman's hair is *blonde*, and – what is more – rather badly dishevelled.'

A poetess in a nightdress, her hair in disarray, throws herself from the window of her bedroom. The nightdress gets caught in the ironwork of the balcony, and the woman remains there, hanging upside-down, her hair stretching desperately like thousands of fingers towards the ground she wanted to reach: a failed, ridiculous suicide. A sweet woman sweetly rejected by a prince chants lewd verses and lets out a piercing laugh, she enters the water in her nightdress, her dishevelled hair is full of flowers, she goes down the river singing at the top of her voice, until the flowers in her hair get inextricably tangled with those of the water plants. And all those beautiful young women in their nightdresses, their bodies arched in front of the cameras of the men come to study them, their eyes rolled back and their hair in disarray, screaming endless insults and blasphemies. And then the women at the Castle, less photogenic, less beautiful than the rest, but still in their nightdresses and still screaming and still tearing out their hair . . .

Cybele's hair is never dishevelled. At the most, a stray wisp. She's in the plane now, her hair piled on top of her head, bending over her papers covered with figures and graphs, ascending and descending curves, from time to time a stray wisp escapes from her chignon, she flattens it against her cheek with one hand while continuing to write with the other. She hasn't looked at her neighbours, she didn't greet them when she sat down, she doesn't even know if they are men or women. She didn't watch the sunset, either, when the plane took off, she hadn't asked for a seat next to the window, that kind of thing doesn't matter to her. She doesn't like travelling in this direction, returning home from abroad, because it causes her to lose six hours. In the opposite direction, she says, it's much better, the day has thirty hours instead of eighteen. If only every day could be as long! Life is too short: the years, months, weeks and days are far too short to do what must be done. Especially if you subtract the hours devoted to sleeping, eating, and public transport. She rebukes me for not reading on the underground.

'How can you just sit there doing nothing? It's so tedious. With a book, you can be transported into another universe. You can learn something and go somewhere at the same time.'

'I learn things on the metro, anyway. I watch people, I listen to them, or else I day-dream. You know, Cybele, day-dreaming can be a form of escape, too; a way of going somewhere else without moving.'

'Yes, but it's so much more limited!'

Cybele never dreams, she says. Neither by day nor by night. Indeed, she sleeps as little as possible. In the plane she will have tried to catch a few hours' rest so as to be up to facing the difficult day ahead. She won't have seen the sunrise. Awakened by the loudspeaker, she'll arrange her hair without looking in the mirror. When it's time to fold up her tray-table for the landing, she'll put away her papers and draw a scientific magazine from her bag. The thought that the plane might crash won't even cross her

27

mind. She finds my fears so childish that I don't tell her about them any more.

'Aren't you afraid of hitch-hiking around all by yourself?'

'No, why should I be afraid?'

'You hear the most horrendous things.'

'Yes, but I always get picked up by men like you, who've heard the most horrendous things and want to keep them from happening to me.'

'Oh! That's good . . . You've been lucky, then.'

'So you entered the coffee-shop, you were alone, it was approximately nine o'clock in the evening, it had been dark for three hours and it was pouring with rain. Is that correct?'

'Yes.'

'Didn't you notice that you were the only woman in the coffee-shop?'

'Yes, I did, but I needed to warm up, I was freezing to death, I didn't know where else to go.'

'What were you wearing?'

'I beg your pardon . . . What did you say?'

'How were you dressed?'

'You were in nightdresses? Both you and Alix?'

'I beg your pardon?'

'So you went out wearing the nightdress that had been lent to you by the Castle.'

'No, I didn't! I didn't steal anything! No one has lodged a complaint for theft, I was wearing my own raincoat, it was cold outside.'

'It's too cold. I don't know if I'll be able to . . .'

28

'I must say she isn't helping matters much.'

'Are you a lesbian?'
'Objection, your Honour. That question bears no relation to the facts under examination.'

Alix will be there. She'll come with the Friends. They will have rented a van for the day. Ten, twenty – no, thirty women packed in tight. Sixty legs and sixty arms intertwined. Loud voices, peals of laughter to bolster up their courage. Chattering, babbling, interrupting each other, inventing slogans . . . whereas within each one of them, fear will have burned a hole of silence. The multi-coloured words serve to hide the hole from other people. All that can be seen is a van bristling with women, their gaiety so raucous they seem to be on their way back from a wild party. Alix is at the wheel. She drives brutally, making each gear whine before switching into the next, braking at the last second before stopping at red lights, taking corners almost without slowing down. The women get tossed back and forth, they fall out of their seats, roll on top of each other and yelp with laughter. The radio is playing love songs that all of them know by heart; they whistle them between their teeth. The lyrics won't come out, the women don't know how to pronounce them any more, the words are engraved in their memories but will never again cross their lips. And so they whistle. Alix whistles, too, when she's not talking to the Friends with her head twisted round to look at them over her shoulder. They tell her to keep her eyes on the road, but for Alix cars just drive themselves. Alix's hands on the steering-wheel. Her hands are dark, large and strong. Like the rest of her.

'Omaya, do you realise we've known each other for

29

almost twenty years? That calls for a celebration!'

Alix has invited the Friends. All of them are here tonight,
in the Flat, it's the month of June, the windows gape onto
the street, the music drowns out the car-horns and the
sirens. The Friends are dancing, imitating flowers, trees
and bird flight with their arms. They are made up and
dressed up with violet- and rose-coloured extravagance:
sequined scarves and eyelids, net stockings showing
through the side slits of full-length dresses, leather
trousers, boots or sandals, cigarette-holders, they are
splendid and carefree, I watch them dance, I love them
and I too begin to dance. Alix is in the kitchen, her hands
are every bit as sure with food as on the steering-wheel,
she pours without measuring, tastes, adds, lights a
cigarette and whistles between her teeth. She's making
chilli. Since she's the one who's making it, there won't be
the agony of the slaughtered animal in every mouthful,
there won't be the memory of spilled blood, eyes popping
from their sockets, meat-grinders crushing flesh, there
will be nothing but beauty, the odours of a sultry country
where all the women dress in red, orange, yellow, the
heaviness of siestas and the frenzy of castanets . . .
Everything will go just fine, until tomorrow morning.
Don't think now of Omaya cleaning out the pot, Omaya's
fingers scratching the hardened blackened meat cemented
to the bottom, I've spent my whole life scrubbing pots, it
won't come off, I'll have to rinse it with hot water and
start again . . . As long as Alix is here, I'm not haunted by
the idea of the water-heater exploding, it's only when
Omaya is alone, the smell of gas, the defective appliance,
the flames leaping higher and higher . . . Conflagration!
Every time the heater lights up with a gasp, I'm convinced
this is the end. A poetess lights the oven in her kitchen,

she is numb with cold, she lights it to get warm and then still warmer, in her head it will never be warm enough, she slips her head inside the oven: roast brain, successful suicide. A woman writer is locked up in a Castle, she has a nervous illness, she wants to be a ballerina but the Lords tell her she must never dance again, ballet gets her too excited, it might make her illness worse. Her husband, a famous writer, uses her letters to fill out and render credible a character in the major novel he is working on. This character is a woman with a nervous illness who has been locked up in a Castle. The woman in the novel gets well after having completely destroyed her husband. The novelist's wife remains locked up in the Castle for many years, until the day the water-heater explodes . . . Conflagration! The ballerina is reduced to ashes, her body is identified by the ballet shoe on one charred foot.

Alix whom I love never thinks about such things. Objects submit to her willingly. Not once have I seen her struggle with a zip. She undresses as she drives: in arabesques, and with evident pleasure. As long as she is here, objects submit to me as well. I'm in a state of grace.

She carries the dishes in one by one, on her head. She does a little dance-step and the others applaud. She takes me in her arms and we dance together. It's like being on stage. Alix always performs this miracle: she turns the Flat into a theatre. It's no longer a place where doubts and dangers lurk, all at once everything seems to me divinely obvious: I know how to talk and how to laugh. Move. Be moved.

'But I don't understand what you're afraid of, Omaya.'
'It can happen anywhere, any time . . . For example, when I went down to buy the beer, at the beginning of the party, a man started following me in the street.'

31

'So what?'

'So . . . I was dressed like this, for you, I was thrilled to be feeling so beautiful, and to think it was finally summer, still light at ten o'clock . . . And then I heard, behind me: Are you alone? And everything collapsed.'

'But why?'

'Because . . . my beauty was no longer destined for you but for a stranger. My dress had changed its meaning, it had become a provocation. My body had changed its meaning, it was no longer mine to give but his to take. Don't you understand?'

'A little, maybe. What was the man like?'

'I don't know, I didn't look at him.'

'Can you describe your assailants?'

'Describe them?'

'What were they like, physically?'

. . .

'Listen, young lady, you claim to have spent more than four hours in their company, so you had ample time to observe them. What were they like? Tall? Short? What colour was their hair? Were they black? Yellow? Red, white, blue? Try to remember.'

'. . . One of them was shorter than the other two.'

'Try to remember. When did you first notice you were in love with your father?'

'I didn't say I was in love with my father, I said I was afraid of him.'

'Fear is often a distorted form of desire, as you know very well. A form the conscious mind finds more acceptable. So this fear – as you put it – when did it start?'

'But what do you mean, darling? You're afraid to drive

32

the car now? You can't come and meet me at the airport because you're afraid?'

'Yes, that's what I said, Cybele.'

'But you know my car, you've driven it dozens of times, what makes you afraid of it, all of a sudden?'

'Do I really have to explain it to you over the telephone? Couldn't you just believe me, for once?'

'Of course I believe you, it's just that . . . I can't believe it! You've always loved to drive.'

'I'll take the bus to the airport, if you need help with your luggage.'

'Oh . . . I'll manage by myself, don't put yourself out.'

'It's not a question of putting myself out. Please don't be angry.'

'I'm not angry, I don't understand, that's all. I'll call you as soon as I get home, okay?'

'Okay.'

Omaya presses the button next to the word 'Basement', the lift doors slide shut in front of her eyes, then slide open onto darkness. Moist grey cement, metallic monsters dozing, concrete coloumns, Examination Room, Examination Room, Omaya advances with the car keys in her right hand.

Don't forget to put a whistle on your key-ring. You should put the key you'll be needing first right next to the whistle, before leaving the house, so as not to waste time looking for it once you're outside. Always hold the key-ring in your right hand, placing the keys carefully between your fingers with the sharp ends out. These are your own personal brass knuckles, a very simple and yet highly effective weapon against possible assailants.

33

Omaya holds the key to the car door between her thumb and index finger. She inserts it in the lock. The key refuses to turn. Stuck. I'll never get out of this garage alive. Omaya removes the key, inserts it the other way round, this time the door opens, I slip in behind the steering-wheel, choose another key and insert it. Ignition, choke, headlights, seat-belt, the car is warming up.

If you've left your car parked in the street, or even in an underground car park, always make sure – *before* opening the door – that there's no one hiding in the back seat.

Omaya backs up slowly, very slowly. The concrete columns loom large, attempt to graze her, and withdraw. The garage door shakes itself and yawns. The car crawls up to the surface, to the light of day. Omaya's knuckles have gone white, her fingers are gripping the steering-wheel so hard. I have to go to Berg, twenty miles outside the city, for an audition. My appointment is for two o'clock, I've left early on purpose so I won't be in a rush. Approaching the main road: traffic. Nothing serious, but the engine is running a bit fast and the temperature gauge has started to rise . . . *Achtung*! No, it isn't touching the red yet, there's no danger yet. Omaya forces herself to look elsewhere, the engine grumbles. The cars surrounding Omaya are immobilised as far as the eye can see. Stuck. Impossible to turn round, go back to the garage and spend the rest of the day in bed. This must be lived through. Omaya switches on the radio. There are no love songs for her, nothing but the angry voices of men, sometimes accompanied by music and sometimes not, she switches off. Behind her a horn honks, she jumps, catches up the two yards she'd fallen behind and sees that now the gauge is touching the red. She turns the key, the motor

34

dies and the gauge drops below zero. Into the white. Omaya's hands no longer belong to her. They slide off the steering-wheel and slither to her lap, two baby birds fallen out of their nest. Sharp glints from windscreens and rear-view mirrors converge from all directions and scratch at Omaya's eyes. Then her head is yanked to the left by a shrill whistle: a policeman is gesticulating furiously at me, he's ordering me to get moving, I haven't got any choice, Omaya turns the key and the gauge leaps immediately into the red, the car is going to catch fire, it's going to explode, the door is locked and I'm tied down by my safety-belt, all around me the other vehicles are snorting and bellowing with impatience.

One o'clock. Now the motorway is in sight, but in order to reach it I have to go through a tunnel. Omaya rummages in her bag, her fingers like so many panicky wings, her eyes fixed on the tail-lights of the car in front of her. She finds a packet of cigarettes, takes one out, puts it between her lips and rummages again. She's looking for a lighter. I've spent my whole life looking for lighters. She gropes at the dashboard, presses the car-lighter, hard – no, it's the choke! – it goes all the way in, no wonder the engine was running so fast, now the temperature will go back down and everything will turn out all right, tonight I'll tell Alix about it and we'll both have a good laugh . . . No. The gauge is still touching the red, Omaya is still in the middle of the tunnel and the car in front of her has braked once again, I can't move, it's going to explode, Omaya's body will splatter the walls, Omaya's eyes are dry and vitreous but her forehead is weeping, fat tears are sliding down her temples and onto her cheeks, Omaya's brain starts thumping against her skull . . . *Alert! Alarm! Achtung!* The siren triggered by her heart tears through Omaya's veins, making every coiled-up nerve vibrate as it goes by.

Quarter past one. The tunnel is over and done with. Suddenly Omaya notices a burning sensation on her thighs. There, the motor's on fire, this time it's true! No, it's just the sun, don't panic, it's nothing but a sunbeam in your lap . . . It can't be the sun, there's smoke, too, oh my God the car is burning . . . Conflagration! Stop it! It's nothing but your own cigarette smoke . . . Omaya parks the car at the edge of the motorway, pours water into the radiator. The water hisses as it touches the white-hot metal. Omaya's hands are still quivering.

If you have a breakdown on the motorway, do not get out of the car. If a man stops and offers to help you, make sure your door is locked and do not open it under any circumstances. At the most, you might roll down your window an inch or two and hand him a note asking him to call a breakdown lorry. If he really wants to help, he'll do just that. If not, you're better off inside your car, even if you have to spend the night there.

While the engine is cooling off, Omaya stretches out in the grass at the side of the road. The flayed virgin. The rabbit . . . No! It was the Owl's fault! . . . He's the one that taught me how to drive. Everything seemed so easy. I can float! I can drive! Seated at first between his legs, I would hold the steering-wheel. When a lorry suddenly loomed up in front of us and a collision seemed inevitable, I'd cover my face with both hands and the Owl would save me from death. As long as he was there, I had nothing to fear.

Half past one. Omaya has turned off the motorway, she's looking for Berg. A road map is spread out on the seat next to her, the theatre is marked with an X. She reads the

36

road signs, follows the arrows, after making many turns arrives at Merg. Berg is no longer indicated anywhere. The sun is burning hot. Omaya pulls up in front of the Merg town hall and gets out of the car. She runs inside to consult a more detailed map of the area. Two men come up on either side of her, caress her with their jokes and their advice – it's because I'm made up for the audition, it's not me they're after, it's the Sorceress, Omaya isn't here – and, rushing off with her mind aboil, even more disoriented than before, she gets back in the car and chooses a road at random. The map beside her has become a meaningless drawing, a child's scrawl. Now on the dashboard, it's the clock that draws her eyes like a magnet: four minutes to two. Three minutes. Two. One.

It is exactly two o'clock when Omaya arrives at the next village, called Lerg, the sun is burning hot, the streets are empty, the shutters are closed, the road signs are covered with gibberish. It is sheer lunacy to be looking for a theatre in countryside like this. Omaya hasn't the slightest recollection of the script she had prepared, her thoughts have gone completely flat, her mind is a huge map littered with unlikely place names and inscrutable itineraries. As she drives away from Lerg, Omaya passes a man going down the road with long strides. She brakes, backs up and opens the door for him. The man gets in beside her. He's a native of the area and his words sound like a hideous poem:

'Do you want to go to Merg or Berg? It's not the same direction at all, Berg and Merg. I live in Lerg, myself, I'm just going to spend the afternoon in Schlerg. But if you want to go to Merg, you'd better turn round . . . Oh, you want to go to Berg, do you? Okay, that's fine then, you just keep going down this road until you get to Terg and then you take a right – wait a minute, no, a left – aren't you afraid of picking men up like this?'

'Afraid?'

'It isn't a very good idea, you know. As it happens, I'm an old man, but there was no way you could have know that from behind. I could have been a prisoner on the run, or else some weirdo . . . Well, this is where I get off, you just keep going straight till you get to Terg, right, got that? Are you okay? You don't look too well . . .'

'You can see that my client is in no condition to confront her assailants.'

'You have nothing to fear within the confines of the court, young lady.'

Nothing to fear any more, we're protected by the four walls. A window in the door, so they can see what we are doing at all times. Just in case we took it into our heads to hang ourselves or slit our wrists. No bars on the windows – impossible to die by throwing yourself from a second-floor window. Down below: dead leaves and grey bushes, no concrete.

A female artist is in love with a male artist – a sculptor with a passion for anagrams. He tells her in a foreign tongue:

> ROSE WITH HEART OF VIOLET.
> VIOLATED HEART DARED TO KILL.
> OPEN THROAT SHALL BE LAW.

He tells her: The body is comparable to a sentence which asks to be decomposed.

In a love letter, he thanks her for: The passion with

38

which you scrupulously dismembered yourself in front of me last night.

He adds that this evening, he would like to: Peel your skin upwards from the rump the length of your back, until it has veiled your face – with the exception of your smile.

With the exception of her smile.

He sculpts and paints and photographs, year after year, disarticulated dolls: amalgamated arms and legs, heads and genitals and breasts.

She falls ill, so they shut her away in a Castle and she writes the story of her illness.

He says he dreams of being able to: Preserve the trace left by a nude who has thrown herself from a window and fallen to the pavement.

She throws herself from a window, scarcely slowed by the pane whose shards of glass accompany her fall. Successful suicide. Lying on the pavement, she manages at last to look like a sculpture of the man she loves.

If you stand on the roof of a house and release, at the same moment, a feather and a spoon, which will reach the ground first? Very good. Now imagine you release a spoon and a knife. Well? Very good. A woman and a shard of glass? Very good.

But it's impossible to throw ourselves out of these rooms, and impossible to lock ourselves inside. They alone have the keys. The same key opens every door in every wing. In the garden, you can distinguish at a distance people who have keys from people who don't by the way they walk. Omaya doesn't have a key. Everyone has the right to look at her through the window. Sitting on her bed, she protects herself behind a smokescreen. Peek through, screw up your eyes . . . but the four walls are bare. In some of the other rooms, women have stuck up posters on the walls with adhesive tape: giant faces of film-stars and singers, or else, more rarely, sketches and watercolours of their own. The walls look even barer that way. Gaping souls, flayed souls. The day I arrived at the Castle, there was a painting of Lorna's hanging on the wall. Lorna is doing much better, the women with keys told me – she's painting, she's showing more of herself. And when they found the painting stuffed behind the radiator: Lorna's not doing so well these days – she's hiding, she's withdrawn.

A woman writer is locked in a bedroom with yellow wallpaper. She has a nervous illness. The Lord has ordered her never to touch pen or paintbrush again. These things make her even more nervous and even more ill. She's the one who has locked the door of her room so that she can tear off the yellow wallpaper in peace – and write in secret. A few years later, chloroform: successful suicide. Here, there is no wallpaper and no one has locked up Omaya. She has nothing to write, nothing to say, they tear the words from her just the same. Like strips of wallpaper, like strips of skin.

'Tell me about this man.'
'He isn't clear.'
'The man who stands above you, leaning over?'
'He isn't clear. I can't raise my eyes to look at him.'
'He wouldn't look like me, by any chance?'
. . .
'The toilet seat, the hot seat? Therapist, the rapist? What do you think?'
. . .
'Since when have you been in love with me?'

40

A very young couple is now sitting in the seat across from Omaya. Simulated black leather, simulated passion. The boy slides his arm all the way round the girl's shoulders so that his wrist is exactly in front of her mouth. Encircling his wrist, a studded leather bracelet. One metal stud in front of each white tooth. He squeezes the girl until her face pivots round to meet his. Tongues, teeth, pimples, hairs, saliva, studs, lipstick: it's a kiss. He releases her. The girl smiles. Her eyes meet Omaya's stare. She glances down, blushes and smiles again. The boy squeezes her. The girl resists. He squeezes harder. The girl's head pivots round and they kiss. Omaya looks out the window at the tunnel walls flashing past. She hears the sucking noises. Her stomach heaves.

'You see that? She's starting to puke. Uuuggh – it's disgusting.'
'Let her go, let her go a second. Let her puke and get it over with. Let go, I said.'
Omaya has eaten nothing all day. She spits up bile, her throat burns and stings. Crouched in the sawdust with her head between her knees, she sees – but very far away, like the sun setting in a winter sky – a scarlet droplet.

'Cybele, I'm scared.'
'Yes, I know, darling. I get scared, too, sometimes, but I'm sure your daddy will come back to us. You'll see. Everything will be just like it was before.'
'Why was his forehead all scratched up this morning?'
'He says he was walking in the forest all night long and the branches slapped him in the face without his noticing.'
'Is that it? Is that why?'
'I don't think so.' .
'Why, then?'

'Well, I think . . . I think he tried to tear his hair out.'
'But *why*, Cybele?'

'Oh darling . . . He's got so many ideas in his head that he just can't make them come out. So his head feels like it's going to explode. And he has to . . . I mean, he tries to . . . It's as though he wanted to open a cage to free the birds inside. Do you understand?'

You're the one who refused to understand, Cybele. Later on, the Owl started taking me with him on his nightwalks. What he was doing in the forest was not opening cages, but smashing everything that bore any resemblance to a limit. One evening we'd taken the car and we came to a barrier. The letters on the sign were perfectly clear: PRIVATE PROPERTY. He was beside himself with rage. Livid, he got out of the car, pushed the barrier aside, and we penetrated into the forbidden territory together. Joy took hold of him and rendered him unrecognisable. No one saw us, no one punished us, the barrier was put back into place as though nothing had ever happened . . . But were the birds free for all that? And later still, when I was locked up in my own cage, did he ever come to help me break the bars? Not once. He won't come today, either. He'll just keep going round the lake, each circuit bringing him a little closer to death. It's as though his rounds were concentric circles getting progressively smaller instead of progressively larger. And when he gets to the middle of the lake, it will be the end. The immobile centre.

> A day is perhaps
> Infinity
> Full stop: that is all.

One of Lorna's poems. The women with keys were

ecstatic: what a blessing! Creative writing has helped her emerge from her private hell! They would put up just about anything on the dining-room walls. Once there was a piteous drawing of a red ship with the following legend: I'm sixty-five years old, almost ready to kick the bucket. The ship had been wrecked on the white page.

If you hold the spoon vertically, it won't float. If you enter the water standing up instead of lying down, you won't float. A woman writer fills her pockets with stones and enters the water standing up. Successful suicide. The waves are real.

> Who died
> Who did
> Who

One of Lorna's poems.

On stage, Omaya says words of love to a man she doesn't love. The man replies with words of feigned tenderness, then feigned jealousy, then feigned anger. He grabs a real dagger and pretends to plunge it into Omaya's heart. Omaya collapses. Every night she collapses after pronouncing the words of love. The dagger is real. The collapse is real. The death is simulated. Night after night, Omaya pretends to die, and everyone applauds.

The knife is as sharp as a razor-blade. Omaya is cutting an onion. I've spent my whole life cutting onions. Behind me, Alix is whistling, she's wearing my apron, we're making a Spanish omelette together for our Sunday lunch, the Flat is a theatre and everything is fine. Omaya sees the knife getting closer, slice by slice, to her fingers holding the onion. The knife is real. It cuts into the fingers: first joint, second, third, then the wrist. The fingers rotate the onion through ninety degrees. The knife repeats its act, cutting first the onion and then Omaya's left hand, there is no pain, not a drop of blood has spilled onto the tiles, Alix hasn't noticed a thing. The knife is real. I could plunge it into Alix's breast, it would be so easy . . . I don't want to! But it would be easy: the knife is here, her throat is there, if I took her in my arms she'd offer up her throat and it would all be over in a second . . . I don't want to! But how can I be sure I won't? All it would take is a moment's distraction . . .

'Where did this sudden wish to cut your friend's throat come from?'
'Not a wish. It didn't come from me but from the knife. I loved her.'
'Love is often a distorted form of hatred, as you know very well. A form the conscious mind finds more acceptable. So tell me, why did you want to eliminate her?'

'Tell me, are you a lesbian?'
'I . . . no. Yes. I mean . . . no.'

Dear Omaya my little angel my great actress my lucky star
You know it's funny but I didn't like the way you collapsed on stage last night at the end of the play, you collapse with too much conviction, it seems to me that the Red Lady is PROUD, a whole lot prouder than that, but what does it matter provided that you get up afterwards and come towards me, whole and perfect, with your arms outstretched . . . Alix

Saroyan opens the door and holds out his arms. Omaya

44

stands straight and rigid, arms glued to her sides. If you remain vertical, you risk nothing. If you give yourself up to the arms of the lake, you can die. No, it's the other way around.

'Come in, come in. I've just made some tea. Are you thirsty?'

'Cold, more than anything else.'

'Here, drink this, it'll warm you up. So . . . you feel like working again, do you?'

'I need to. It's so cold, Saroyan.'

'Yes. But . . . you're sure you're feeling better? You've got over it?'

. . .

'I can't tell you what it did to me. I wanted to kill them. I could have killed them . . .'

. . .

'You don't feel like talking about it?'

'Interrogations on all sides.'

'I understand. Enough of that, then. Go on, drink up – you must get your strength back. Poor dear.'

'No.'

'Come over to the Theatre tomorrow. We're in the middle of casting. There'll be something for you. You're sure it's . . . it's not too soon?'

'I'm not sure of anything.'

'Let me give you the script, that way you can look over the women's roles and see what appeals to you.'

Omaya flips through the pages. The words of love blur beneath her eyes.

'It's not easy . . .'

'How about if we cued each other a bit, sitting right here on the bed, the way we used to? I'll put on a record.'

'No . . . it's getting late, it'll be dark soon.'

'It's only eight o'clock! Listen, you must try to get over

this. I'm your friend. Remember me?'

. . .

'Omaya. Remember? I'd never do anything to hurt you. Don't you trust me any more?'

Saroyan clasps her face between his hands. His own face approaches. A mask. Thick lips, whiskers, nostrils. Omaya screams. The same gestures. Love is often a distorted form of hatred. The same gestures. Madly in love. The same gestures. Madly in hate. Removing clothes, kissing, caressing, loving. Removing clothes, kissing, caressing, hating. Life, death. The same gestures. My wife is pregnant, your Honour.

The Wives are in the bus, together. In the bus one must give up one's seat to pregnant women. The Wives are perpetually pregnant. Between the three of them, they've brought fourteen kids into the world. They will have hired someone to look after them today. This kind of thing is not for children. It has nothing to do with children. The children have been kept completely in the dark. They've been told that their fathers have a bone to pick with their employer at the garage. They're taking him to court. Children must not be told the whole truth. We know the whole truth, though. The truth is that men are nothing but grown-up children. One has to be aware of that, and conduct oneself accordingly.

The Wives support each other. They boost each other's egos, curl each other's hair, drink each other's coffee. Sitting around each other's kitchen tables, they spend their mornings chatting. They understand each other. In the bus, two Wives are sitting side by side. Their thighs flattened against the seat form a single thick carpet of soft flesh. Their plump knees rub against the knees of the Wife sitting opposite. Their six lips move ceaselessly. They were carefully reddened before the departure. In each of the three bags there is a hand-mirror and a tube of lipstick, just in case the first layer doesn't hold out until noon. Another tube, a black one, for the eyes, just in case tears are shed. A packet of tissues to wipe away the streaks of black. But no tears will be shed. Everything will go just fine. Daddy will come home again. Don't worry, dear. Everything will turn out all right. Everything will be just as it was before. And an overstuffed wallet: bus tickets, kiddie snapshots, banknotes brought home by the daddies in question. And a comb, just in case the waves sculpted by the curlers get ruffled by the wind. And a list of things to buy on the way home, for the holiday feast.

'I was thinking of lamb. What about you?'

'Oh, chicken, I should think. And you?'

'Me? Rabbit. My husband loves rabbit.'

The thing is, there are girls especially for that. Girls just for fun. Girls just for fooling around. The thing is, they'd spent the evening drinking. After a bit of booze, men are more like grown-up children than before. They won't listen to reason, they just fool around with whatever comes to hand. The lucky thing is, they happened on a lunatic. Otherwise they would have been in hot water. But the girl is raving, it's been proved that she was raving before it happened. We must latch onto that, we must repeat it until everyone believes it. They're obliged to take our word over that of a sick actress. The girl is raving, she says the first thing that comes into her head. She's the one who insisted, they're the ones who refused. She got mad and started screaming, all they did was slap her face to calm her down. They got home before midnight. That's the way it happened. Those are the facts. Yes, they do tend to fool around when they've been drinking, it's happened before. They do get carried away sometimes, that's true, they won't listen to reason. They're just like grown-up children. The children need their fathers, and so do we. How are we supposed to buy food for them? It's hard enough as it is.

The Wives are frightened. Their words give them courage and face. Raving . . . booze . . . lunatic . . . fool around . . . raving . . . booze . . . lunatic. The same words over and over again. Table . . . chair . . . desk . . . window . . . table . . . chair . . . table.

Omaya has climbed onto the table, her body is being tossed about by the music from the juke-box. Even with her eyes closed she can sense the worried expression on Saroyan's face. But he's mistaken, there's nothing wrong, it's just that I'm so happy tonight. I know the owner of this coffee-shop, he won't hold it against me. The other customers are watching me, too. I'm dancing beautifully, they like it, I'm so happy.

Saroyan has gone and unplugged the juke-box. He's coming back towards me, his eyes are black with worry, he takes my hand, helps me gently off the table and sits me down on a chair.

'Aren't you feeling well? What came over you?'

'Yes, I am feeling well, for once.'

'Omaya, you are not in a theatre. A table is not a stage. What's the matter? Have you had too much to drink?'

'That was my favourite song. What gives you the right to cut it off?'

'Don't shout. Everyone's looking at us. Please get a grip on yourself, you're making us look ridiculous.'

The word falls over Omaya like a black shroud. She crumples beneath it: her arms on the table, her head on her arms, ridicule on her head. In front of her eyes, a tiny cup filled with toothpicks. Pointed stakes. You spread apart the thighs of the lamb, you shove in the stake, you push, you laugh with terror, the stake penetrates the anus, it advances with difficulty along the spinal column, you can see the bump moving forward like a mole burrowing along the surface of the ground, you push, the flesh distends, it mustn't tear, the stake goes in deeper, you laugh with terror, and at last, after a final struggle around the thorax, the point of the stake emerges from the throat, you keep pushing until the two ends of the stake, on either side of the animal, are of equal length . . . Omaya gets up slowly, she picks up the cup of toothpicks, goes over to the next table and picks up the cup on it as well, she goes around the coffee-shop picking up all the toothpick cups, politely, after asking permission from the dumbfounded customers – and what was Saroyan doing all that time? I haven't the slightest recollection – and then, holding the twenty-odd tiny cups in the crook of her left arm, she heads for the ladies' room.

All the stakes in the water! Every which way, tumbling madly, like when the giant tree-trunks go floating down the river and get stuck in a bend, start piling up, smashing into one another . . . Log jam! Pile-up! Traffic jam! *Achtung!*

Omaya flushes the toilet.

'I suppose you forgot to do your homework again?'
'No, I did it . . .'
'Look at that mess. It's nothing but mumbo-jumbo. When are you going to start taking school seriously, Omaya? You don't pay any attention in class, you don't even try to concentrate, you're always clowning around. You think you're smart? You're completely ridiculous. This won't do at all, you know. I'm going to have to have a talk with your mother.'

49

'I don't understand, Omaya. Look at these marks. What's gone wrong? Until this year you never had the slightest problem at school, and suddenly you've started going downhill. You fool around during lessons, you imitate the teacher, she tells me you've become the class clown.'

'It's because school bores me this year, and the teacher's out to get me . . . The other kids are bored, too, only they don't have the nerve to say so. I like to make them laugh once in a while.'

'Don't tell me that school bores you, that's ridiculous. There's always something you can learn, no matter who your teacher is. Look at me, I've never stopped learning – I learn something new every day. All you have to do is pay attention, be on the look-out, stay alert to the world around you at all times.'

'Er . . . Robert, isn't it?'

'Well, well! What a surprise!'

'I thought it must be you.'

'My goodness! I don't know if I would have recognised you.'

'How are you doing?'

'Fine, just fine . . .'

'What have you been up to? You've changed offices?'

'That's right. I work in a different neighbourhood now. And it's not exactly the same job as before.'

'You got promoted?'

'Exactly. A year ago.'

'Congratulations! So what kind of work are you doing now?'

'Oh . . . you know . . .'

'In the marketing field, is it?'

'Yes, that's it, more or less: surveys, advertising, getting

50

things in shape, ship-shape as it were, speculating, specularising, statisticising.'

'Artificial intelligence?'

'That, too, from time to time, data processing sessions, computations, computerisations, we make an effort to flush out ridicule wherever it takes refuge, to eliminate possible failures, insecurities and evil tongues to the best of our abilities. What about you – still in the same place?'

'Haven't budged.'

'Don't you get a bit bored sometimes?'

'Who, me? Oh, no, you know . . . I'm not the ambitious type . . . This is my stop – got time for a coffee?'

'Awfully sorry, I have an important meeting at ten sharp. Maybe next time. Bye for now!'

'All right, see you.'

Omaya looks out of the window at the tunnel walls flashing past. Cybele never looks out of windows, she says you can't learn anything from the countryside. The countryside isn't human, only what is human is worthy of interest, and that's more than enough, it's inexhaustible. She says: You can't imagine how complex the human brain is, it's a veritable miracle, a most extraordinary machine. Take my aeroplane, for instance, the one I was in last night on my way to join you, I was inside the plane, and yet the plane itself had originally been inside a man's head. Man's distinctive characteristic is imagining things that surpass him. You have a lot of imagination, too, only you don't know how to use it constructively yet – to shape reality. Imagination alone isn't enough. I'm not questioning your gifts as an actress, that goes without saying, it's just that . . . If only you worked in films, at least there'd be something left over at the end. With the theatre, as soon as a show is finished, it disappears and it's as though you'd created nothing at all. I'm sure that must be why you're feeling a bit gloomy these days. You're in between shows, you're floating, your head feels empty – but that's perfectly understandable!

Cybele understands nothing. She only talks because she can't decently go away yet; she's trying to make the time allotted for our visit go by faster. Usually, when there's something she doesn't want to see, she can protect herself behind a book or a magazine. Here, there's no way she can avert her eyes. We're walking in the garden and she's forced to contemplate all these people without keys, it makes her dreadfully uncomfortable, so she keeps her eyes on me, she lectures me, it uses up the minutes and appeases her conscience at the same time.

'Why don't you say anything?'

'I have nothing to say.'

'It's okay with you just to stay here surrounded by all these wrecked lives?'

'Yes, it's okay with me.'

'Don't say that, Omaya, it hurts me terribly. Don't you even want to get out? After all, you can leave whenever you like. Answer me, for heaven's sake. Don't you want to leave?'

'No, Cybele. I – do – not – want – to – leave.'

'But what's wrong with you? Are you on drugs? They've stuffed you with tranquilisers, is that it? You sound like a sleepwalker.'

Cybele is all tied up in knots, her features distorted by anxiety, I cannot help it, I want her to go away.

'You still haven't said anything.'

'Go away, Cybele, please. Go away.'

'Why don't you say anything?'

'My brain is coagulated, the words can't get out.'

'Why do you always speak in terms of coagulation? Words are not blood, after all. The mouth is not an open wound through which language oozes. What might be the origin of that image, do you think?'

'You'll have to speak up when you answer their questions. Sound convincing – try not to hesitate. Look them in the eye, show them you can face up to them.'
'Are they going to start from the beginning again? "Why did you leave the Castle?" '
'Yes. We have to take it from the top, every single time. But try not to let it bother you. Just talk as loudly and as firmly as you can – as though you were on stage.'

'The point of mask work is to force you to dispense with language. To help you discover the expressive possibilities of your body, all the messages it's capable of transmitting without recourse to words. You'll be working with a different mask each week. The casting will be completely arbitrary. Each of you will play, in turn, the Clown, the Owl, the Chicken, the Sorceress, the Vamp, and so forth. At first you'll work all by yourself in front of the mirror, and then in pairs. The idea is to bring your bodies into total agreement with the mask. To find and internalise the appropriate gestures, tics, and physical habits. Your own face will be of no help to you; this means you'll literally have to change metabolisms, undergo a complete metamorphosis. To achieve this, you must become intimately acquainted with the past history of the mask. What experiences have led it to adopt this particular grimace rather than another? What memories are engraved in its mind and body? You'll have to invent these memories in as much detail as possible, and make them yours. Evoke them over and over until the corresponding movements have become natural to you. Then, little by little, interaction with other characters can begin. What would an Owl have to say to a Sorceress? How would the Vamp behave in the presence of the Clown? And so forth. Go ahead, choose your masks for the week – you'll be familiar with all of them by the end anyway.'

Above the mantelpiece, in the Flat–Theatre bedroom, a looking-glass. On the mantelpiece, two candle-holders. Omaya has lit the candles. Alix is already in bed, she's waiting for me to join her. The shadows play over Omaya's face reflected in the glass. They deform her features, deepening the rings beneath her eyes, emphasising her wrinkles, damaging her skin. Omaya watches herself age. She holds her breath. Thirty-five years old, forty, fifty, sixty, seventy . . . Her skin cracks, her cheeks sag, her eyes sink into their sockets, her hair whitens, her wrinkles branch out into a spiderweb that gets denser by the second. Omaya laughs with terror and recognises the grimace of her granny. She turns towards Alix and moves across the room with tiny steps, her arms outstretched. She manages to say: Alix . . . and her own voice sounds far away and feeble to her ears.

'Come to bed, angel. I'm almost asleep.'

'Alix, where are you? I can't see a thing . . .'

'Come on. Please. I don't feel like playing games.'

I can't find the bed. I'm fumbling through a fog as tangible as cotton. The cotton hinders my movements, blocks my throat and nostrils, I can hear Alix calling me but how will I ever find her? My name bounces back and forth between two mountain peaks, whereas I am down in the valley, stifled by this fog . . .

Someone grabs me by the shoulders, shakes me, slaps my face.

'Stop screaming, do you hear?'

Someone grabs me by the shoulders, shakes me, slaps my face.

'I can certify that when she came in for examination, there were bruises on her face, chest and stomach. In addition, there was a tear . . .'

The stake advances along the spinal column. The flesh distends, it mustn't tear.

'Why did you refuse to undergo the medical examination ordered by the court?'

'I'm sorry . . . Could you repeat the question?'

'Why did you refuse to write this examination?'

'I'd come to the wrong room. It wasn't that examination I was supposed to write – THE CHALLENGE OF EDUCATION. I hadn't studied anything like that, I'd been called up for a different examination.'

'What exactly had you studied?'

'Theatre . . .'

'And you'd already worked as an actress, is that correct?'

'Yes.'

'You therefore had a certain amount of experience in dissimulation, exaggeration – in a word, telling lies?'

'Omaya, you'll drive me to despair. When are you going to learn to tell the truth? Knowing you take money from my wallet hurts me a lot less than knowing you lie to me. What did you want the money for?'

. . .

'Answer me! What were you going to do?'

Someone grabs me by the shoulders, shakes me, slaps my face.

'You're going to answer me. You're going to tell me the truth.'

'I wanted to buy some lipstick.'

'Lipstick? What for? So you could play the clown again, is that it?'

'Will you stop playing the clown!'

Alix is white with rage. I can see her now. I'm on the bed and she's leaning over me. She slaps my face. I know it's Alix and I know it's for my own good. Panting. Gasping.

'Stop it, Alix. Please. I can't breathe.'

'For the love of God, what came over you? You terrified me!'

'Don't look at me like that. Oh, please don't . . . You're turning into ⸗ . .'

'What am I turning into?'

'Oh no! . . . Your face . . .'

'What's the matter with my face? You're not going to start that again, are you? Omaya, stop it! Are you having a bad dream or what? Wake up! What's the matter with my face?'

'Alix . . . You're not . . . you're not a woman.'

'I'm really going to lose my temper if you keep on like this. Stop it this instant.'

'. . . You're a man.'

And she gets dressed, her gestures firm and sure and quick, and she'll never set foot in the Flat again, and the Flat will never be a Theatre again, and everything will be just as it was before, but worse than before, the water-heater, the oven, the explosions, the conflagrations, the suicides . . . Today Alix will come, she'll be driving the van, whistling between her teeth, twisting her head round to talk to the Friends, and she'll laugh out loud. If I look at her during the trial she'll smile at me. All of them will smile, they'll make gestures of encouragement with their hands. To give people courage, you make a fist and then you raise your arm like a boxing champion, that means you're strong, you know how to defend yourself, you're not afraid of anything or anyone. All the Friends will shake their fists, they'll come into the courtroom singing a song of insolent puns at the top of their voices, their right hands will be raised and their left hands will be joined in a chain of violets and roses. Those will be the only splashes of colour on the whole stage, they'll be surrounded by the navy-blue or black-and-white costumes of the other actors, a shadowy threatening mass: the swarm of uni-formed policemen, rigid and alert, furtively caressing their truncheons, the judge, the public prosecutor and the lawyers, women metallicised by ambition, all dressed in black, all dressed in power, even Anastasia will have adopted this disguise so as to pass unnoticed, she'll seem distant, almost foreign to me . . . And then, on this dark and motionless background, the Friends will start to dance. They'll go spinning around the courtroom, weaving a net with their arms, and then they'll catch me in the net – as gently as a butterfly – and waft me, carry me far, far away, their arms like a fantastic patchwork in which I shall huddle up and cuddle up until all of us are out of danger . . .

If you feel in danger in the street, scream: Fire! If you hear someone trying to force the lock on your front door, scream: John! Go and get the rifle! If you live alone, keep it a secret. Use a man's name in the phone directory and on your letter-box. But it's far better not to live alone, and not to go out in the streets alone, especially at night; this is nothing but common sense.

And in the metro what can you do, what can you scream? In the underground, shut up or be shut up. Like that Oriental girl last summer, her black hair pulled back in a ballerina bun, her profile almost painfully delicate, like chiselled porcelain . . . She leaned against one of the metal poles, encircling it with a naked leg, I shivered to see her skin in contact with the cold steel . . . And then, all of a sudden, the white porcelain turned bright red: I saw a distinct line of red wash upwards over her face, as a wave washes upwards over the shore, until it had covered her forehead. I even saw the black hairs at the nape of her neck bristle under the impact of the tide of blood; she quickly put her foot down on the floor and turned her back to me, and I just had time to see, on the tip-up seat she'd been facing the second before, the thing – red as well, but soft – disappearing into the flies of a pair of trousers . . . The train came to a halt and the girl got off, her fragile throat constricted, her jugular vein throbbing, wearing her beauty like some kind of taint or leprosy.

She gets into a different carriage, this time she holds the pole with her hand, her eyes are riveted to the floor, and then a man's hand glides slowly down the pole and glues itself to hers, she moves her hand, the other hand follows, slips on top of hers and covers it completely . . . She releases the pole and hunches up against the back of a seat, trying desperately to rid her body of its litheness, stiffening her legs from calves to buttocks so as not to be drawn into the swaying movements of the crowd, and then she feels a palm pressed flat against her thigh, she freezes like an intricate machine whose inner workings have gone awry and jammed, she's incapable of turning round, of even trying to find out what face corresponds to this moist member, the hand grows more insistent, more explicit, gliding upwards towards her crotch, the train stops, the girl gets off . . . she won't get on again. She'll walk along the platform, wending her way through the crowd, anonymous hands will brush her at every step, she'll dodge them for the thousandth time, for the fifty thousandth time, she'll hear the piteous murmurs, the same words over and over, hey pussy, wanna suck me off, lemme ram it up your ass, and then again hey pussy, and gradually the porcelain, instead of fragile, will become friable.

She hears: What a charming smile! – and her teeth clatter to the ground. With bleeding gums, hollow cheeks, amorphous lips, she goes on walking. She hears: What gorgeous hair! – and her shining black tresses detach themselves from her scalp, turn into greying tufts which she tears out by the handful. She hears: My, what beautiful eyes! – and she goes blind. Covering her empty sockets with one hand, she uses the other to feel her way along the corridors of the metro. Then she hears: What luscious legs! – and finds herself a legless cripple.

What a wreck! She still attracts people's attention, but this attention is even more malevolent than before: the unspeakable mixture of pity, disgust and contempt which people of integrity reserve for those who have disintegrated. She'll join ranks with the beggars in the corridors, and finish off, in their company, whatever time is left for her to live – or rather, time will finish *her* off . . .

I've just killed her. Omaya did it. She killed her.

Why did you wish to cut your best friend's throat?

Dear Omaya, my friend, my new incomparable friend
It means so much to me that you've come to stay in my life, do you know that two people who love each other can

59

never be alone, I think of you constantly and it makes me
want to shout from the rooftops, I'm not sad to be
travelling without you, I dream about all the trips we'll be
taking together and I let go of the steering-wheel to clap
my hands for joy . . . Alix

I'm sitting between the Owl's knees. I'm holding the
steering-wheel. We're in the forest, at dusk and at peace. I
know how to drive, I'm really grown-up now, he talks to
me like a grown-up, my hands have replaced his hands, we
form a single body.

Scarcely a shadow. There – up ahead – quick – now –
straight ahead: the sketch of a grey line between the
bushes and the road. The sky is mauve. Shock thud. Dull
short. What is it? The Owl brakes. Omaya is thrown
against the wheel. Honk. What is it? The car has come to a
stop at the edge of the road. It's a rabbit. Omaya's just run
over it. No! He did it! His foot on the accelerator, then on
the brake, too late. He did it! Omaya's holding the
steering-wheel. Shock. The sketch of a grey line. Dull
thud. Shadow. It's a rabbit. The sky is mauve. The Owl
sets Omaya on the grass, he walks back down the road a
bit, bends over and then lifts his head: It's a rabbit. She's
dead. Omaya's killed her. He did it! He's the one who
picked her up by her two hind legs and brought her back
towards me, dangling upside-down, suspended from the
balcony by her nightdress, rigid in death. A movement.
Scarcely a shadow. I saw her. I didn't see her. He braked.
No more movement. The car has come to a stop. He lifts
his head: it's a rabbit. She's dead. He brings her back and
lays her in the trunk on a sheet of plastic. There is no
blood. No pain. She didn't even wriggle. Short shock.
Eyes popping out of their sockets. Torn from their
sockets. Rigid body dangling upside-down. He did it!

Blood pouring from the empty sockets. He did it! The Owl's the one who flayed her, tearing off the strips of skin, peeling the skin upwards from her rump the length of her back, he's the one who chopped her into pieces for a stew, he's the one who licked his chops. Omaya sees nothing of all this. She's curled up in bed, shivering, her head spinning, neon lights before her eyes. Don't you want anything to eat? A thigh? A bit of liver? The heart that's ceased to beat?

In the city she walks fast, shoulders hunched, eyes on the ground. She crosses the street at top speed. Scarcely a shadow, the sketch of a line. Beep, beep! She starts and spins around, a man is smiling at her. He waves. She doesn't know him. He knows her, his smile says. The man knows everything about Omaya. His eyes chop her into pieces. She crosses the street endeavouring to hold the pieces together. She's forgotten how to walk. Theoretically all you have to do is put one foot in front of the other, but what about the rest? – the arms that fail to restore the body's balance when the weight shifts from one foot to the other, the head that constantly threatens to fall to one side, dragging you to the ground . . . Beep, beep! She starts. Smile. Dismembering. Learning to walk again, with greater difficulty each time.

Alix makes fun of me.
    'You do get carried away sometimes, angel.'
    Alix and Omaya are walking down the road, arms round each other's waists. They're in the forest, at dusk and at peace. Their voices are low, from time to time they laugh, I'm so happy. And then, behind them: the sound of a bicycle. The man on the bike goes by, twisting his head round to ogle them. Fifty yards or so down the road he

61

stops, makes a full turn, and passes them coming the other way. Stops, makes a full turn, and passes them again. And again. Omaya has fallen silent. She hears the sound of the bicycle growing louder and softer, louder and softer. Alix acts as if nothing were happening, she goes on talking.

'I can't listen to you, Alix . . . I'm frightened.'

'Frightened? Of him? No. Is that it?'

'Yes . . . I can't help it . . . What if he has a knife?'

'What on earth would he do with a knife? There are two of us and one of him.'

Above all, avoid going out alone.

'My client was alone, there were three of them. If she'd put up a serious resistance, she could have been killed.'

If you get stung by three different hornets, you can die. Can you die if you get stung three times by the same hornet? Or does its venom grow weaker with each sting? The buzzing comes to a halt, the sting is thrust beneath the skin, the hornet ejects its poison and withdraws. Paralysis gradually invades every part of the body. The needle is thrust beneath the skin, it ejects its poison and withdraws. Paralysis gradually invades every part of the mind, the brain's buzzing comes to a halt. The pneumatic drill eviscerates the earth, the bit is thrust beneath the skin of the city and its deafening vibrations tear the air apart. There is no way to defend oneself against that.

Alix is exasperated. She draws up short in the middle of the road, blocks the bike and grabs the handle-bars, forcing the man to get off.

'Listen, you like riding your bike, don't you? Don't you? And we like taking nice quiet walks. So if you don't let us take a nice quiet walk, we won't let you ride your bike. Is that clear? Got it?'

Hesitation. Their eyes wrestle. And then the man – a
very young man as it turns out, almost a boy – gets back
on his bike and speeds away. Alix bursts out laughing. She
comes back towards me, puts both arms around me.

'Is that better? You're not frightened any more?'

'No, I suppose not . . . But I'd just as soon we went back
to the hotel right away. It's starting to get dark.'

The vulnerable points of a man's body, starting from the
top, are as follows: the ears, the nose, the Adam's apple,
the solar plexus, the crotch, the shins, the feet. Don't
forget that your own feet, as well as your nails and teeth,
can be valuable weapons. However, if you do decide to
kick, never raise your whole leg at once. Just raise your
knee and give small, sharp, repeated kicks, either with the
point of your shoe, or – if he's grabbed you from behind –
with your stiletto heel. Otherwise, he could take ad-
vantage of your leg being raised to knock you off your
balance and throw you to the ground. If he's covered your
mouth with his hand, try to pull apart his second and third
fingers with your own fingers; that hurts and will force
him to let go, at least temporarily. But whatever you do,
never forget the basic rule: if you decide to use physical
resistance, it must be *total* and take place within *ten
seconds*, at most, from the time of the attack.

'Come on, get a move on. We told you we'd drive you
back to the Castle. We gave you our word of honour. And
we are men of honour – eh? Aren't we? All we want to do
is look at you. First we have a look, and then we drive you
back. Okay?'

Beneath the white neon, Omaya is struggling with the
buttons on her shirt. I've spent my whole life struggling

63

with buttons. A thread has got tangled round the top one. Omaya's fingers are numb, I'm so cold, I'll never be warm again, I can't catch the thread, time has congealed, it will be the month of December for ever and the button will for ever refuse to come undone.

'Hurry up! We aren't going to wait all night. Get a move on, dammit!'

The hall is overheated. In an arabesque, the woman undoes her brassiere and tosses it into the audience. Applause. The woman is dancing. A spotlight is following her, all the gazes converge upon her. The woman is beautiful. The light is hot. The headlights . . . No, those lights are cold, besides the headlights weren't even on, it was dusk, it was the Owl's fault, he's the one who braked too late and she was killed instantly, she didn't even wriggle . . . The woman wriggles, in an arabesque she unties the ribbons that hold her panties up, removes the panties and tosses them into the audience. Applause. The music accelerates, lubricates, the woman wriggles faster. Droplets of sweat run down everyone's forehead and converge into rivulets, rivers of sweat pour onto the stage. The woman gives herself up to the waves. She smiles, her moist mouth half open. Blinded by the spotlight, she can see nothing – but she hears, in the spaces between notes: panting. The woman undoes the suspenders on her left thigh and starts to roll down her stocking while continuing to dance. Applause. The stocking rolls down the length of her leg, revealing a knee, a calf and finally a foot. Does she then remove her pointed stiletto-heeled shoe, so as to be able to take the stocking completely off? Does she then slip the shoe back on her bare foot? I don't know. The whole thing is nothing but arabesques, applause, spotlights, sweat, and rolling drums. Whatever she does to the left leg, she does the same to the right, and then the suspender-belt itself sails through the air. Ovation. Now the woman is stark naked but for her pointed stiletto-heeled shoes and the triangle of white pearls covering the triangle of black hairs covering the nothingness. Black-out. The dancer vanishes behind the curtain and runs to pick up her cheque. The house lights come up. Well-dressed women can be seen engaged in polite conversation with men who are adjusting their trousers and calling for champagne. Everything flows: the money, the alcohol, the sweat and the rest. Streaks of red and black, streaks of creamy white.

Cybele never uses make-up. Artificial intelligence, natural body. That's why I had to steal money from her to buy lipstick, otherwise I would have stolen her lipstick. Later on, directly from the store: sticks of red and orange and pink and blue and black. Creams of white and beige and brown. Spray-cans and curlers. I lock the bathroom door, just in case Cybele should come home unexpectedly. But Cybele never comes home unexpectedly. In actual fact, the only thing Cybele ever does unexpectedly is leave. See you soon, my little Omaya. You'll have to take care of your daddy all by yourself now. I know you'll manage fine, I know I can trust you. She kisses me and flies away . . .

Fill in the line above your eyelashes, always starting from the inside of the eye and proceeding outwards. Put the rouge on your cheekbones first, to make your face look angular, and then on the chin to create a balanced effect. If you forget your rouge, you can always pinch your cheekbones firmly to make the blood rush to your face. If necessary, you can tear off a bit of skin with tweezers to

65

make the blood flow. Before reddening your lips, draw in the contour using a pencil of the same colour and, if possible, the same brand as your lipstick. If you have moles, it is not obligatory to conceal them beneath your foundation. You can even darken them in with your eyeliner – this will make your beauty more original. Pluck your eyebrows carefully at least once a week. False eyelashes are to be advised against except for those who really need them, such as albinos or very light redheads. If you do wear false eyelashes, never forget to take them off before going to bed and – very important – before crying. Last but not least: every morning when you wake up, use a special lotion to prevent rings beneath your eyes – this procedure should be as automatic as brushing your teeth.

Cybele says that if I keep drawing black lines all over my eyes, I'll damage the skin of my eyelids – and in the long run, my vision. I won't be able to see in the dark any more. I won't be my father's daughter any more. He bequeathed me his owl's eyes and I am ruining them.

The Owl is taking a nap. Omaya plucks her eyebrows carefully. The tweezers plunge into the pupils. She puts blue shadow on the lids and sequins beneath the brows. She piles her hair on top of her head and holds back its rippling cascade with one hand. I still had long hair then. Eyes half shut, she studies her profile through mascara-ed lashes. She is beautiful. Breathtakingly beautiful. The child star. OMAYA. In neon lights. People have to stand in line for hours to see her films. What an amazing woman-child! May we take your photograph, Miss? I won't take up much of your time: could I have your autograph? Money flows in. Omaya gives herself up to the waves. She flies everywhere, visiting countries Cybele has never set foot in. Cybele is green with envy. I send her money so that she can come and join me. She sits in on my rehearsals, my costume fittings, my hair appointments. She shakes her head incredulously: Who would have thought that I'd see my little girl, the one who never wanted me to cut her fringe, in the hands of the world's best hair specialists?

The women without keys go to the beauty parlour as often as they can. It's designed to look exactly like the parlours in the city: on a low table, glossy magazines overflowing with make-up and diet advice; on a high shelf, beauty products lined up like soldiers. The women without keys are allowed one shampoo per week and one haircut per month. The hairdresser, Suzanne, is sweet and generous. Every day she compliments them on their appearance. She even agrees to paint their faces, knowing full well that her work will be spoiled within the half-hour by threads of saliva on chins, forgetful fingers on cheeks, fists rubbing eyes. Omaya goes to the beauty parlour every morning just to watch Suzanne work. She never looks in the mirror any more, cannot bear the idea of hands so much as touching her.

'Where are you headed?'
'To the city centre.'
'Get in . . . Aren't you afraid of hitch-hiking around all by yourself?'
'Who, me? No, why? . . . Should I be?'
'Not with me, but you couldn't know beforehand who was going to pick you up. There are lots of weirdos . . .'
'Up until now I've always been picked up by people like you, who've wanted to protect me from the weirdos.'
'Oh! That's good . . . You're not a shy one, are you?'
And then his hand. My knee. His hand on my knee.

67

'Stop the car, I'm getting out.'

'We're still a long way from the city centre.'

'Stop, I said. Right now!'

'Take it easy . . . There's nothing to get excited about.'

His foot on the accelerator. The brake too late. Will never come again. It's a rabbit. She's dead.

'You don't have to scream! Jesus Christ, are you crazy or something? Get out, then, you little . . .'

'Stop the car. I want to get out.'

'I know a little coffee-shop right near here. We'll just have a drink and then we'll drive you back.'

'No. I prefer to get out right away. I don't feel well.'

'Listen. It's pouring with rain, everything's closed, there are no more buses at this time of night.'

'I'll take a taxi.'

'You told us you were broke. We'll be your taxi for tonight.'

'I have a friend who lives just down the street, I'll go and spend the night at her place.'

'Stubborn, aren't you? That's enough, you'll do as you're told.'

Omaya stretches her hand out towards the door. Never lean out of a moving train. And then his hand. My cheek. His hand on my cheek.

'Are you crazy or something? *Now* are you going to hold still?'

In the street: car horns. Cacophony. Omaya spins around, her eyes popping out of their sockets. Who's dead? The heart that's ceased to beat . . . No, it's only a wedding. In the back seat of the car: a woman in white squeezed in between two men in black. The man at the wheel is leaning on the horn with all his might.

Pandemonium. *Alarm! Alert! Achtung!* The siren screams:
Fire! The Castle burns, the woman who wanted to dance
is reduced to ashes. If you feel threatened in the street,
scream: Fire!

'Screaming won't do you any good. No one can hear
you. You'll be much better off if you're nice to us.'

I've got a seat but Alix is standing up. We're together
without touching, without looking at each other, we're in
love. And then – above me, behind me – this time I'm sure
of it. This time it's true. I can feel him. He's there. He's
really there. I can't see him, I can't turn round, Omaya's
neck is like a concrete column, but I know he's there. I'm
not dreaming. And then his hand. My shoulder. His hand
on my shoulder. No. Now's the time to react. Twist the
column. Unblock the tongue. Jump to my feet. And then
– no – Alix has given him a shove – and he – his rage – his
hand clenching into a fist . . . Omaya turns round slowly in
her seat, as though trapped in a slow-motion shot in a
film, whereas the tussle behind her is wildly speeded up,
and before Omaya has got to her feet, Alix has already
been flung halfway across the carriage, she's already
fallen amongst the other passengers, the train's already
stopped, the man's already disappeared, was he ever even
there, the other people are calmly flipping through their
newspapers, looking out the windows at the tunnel walls
flashing past . . . So what is Alix doing on the floor? And
why is she weeping blood? And I wasn't able to . . .

'Alix . . .'
'Let's forget the whole thing.'
'No . . . You've got to understand. You shouldn't
have . . .'

69

'It doesn't matter, it's all over now. You don't have to thank me.'

'I don't want to thank you . . . I think I'm angry.'

'Oh, that's nice. You're angry.'

'Yes . . . because, you see . . . I should have been the one to . . . to take care of it. I needed to.'

'You couldn't budge. You were petrified. I saw you. I saw red. I lost control.'

'Yes, but . . . but you prevented *me* from doing anything. It was up to me to do something. Otherwise, I'll never get over this. Don't you understand?'

'Yes . . . Yes, I do understand. Omaya. I'm sorry. I'm so sorry.'

I loved her so much. I told her: I'll never cheat on you with anyone but my illness, do you know that? And she answered: Yes, I do. I told her: I love you with all my strength . . . and with all my weakness, do you know that? And she answered: Yes, I do. And then the weakness started getting the upper hand, and I started loving her only because she was strong, and the stronger she got the weaker I got, and she didn't love me any more . . .

Dear Omaya. I stuck my cigarette through all the Os. Everywhere she'd traced my initial: a burned hole. Letters riddled with holes. Letters gone up in smoke. Conflagration! A female writer and a male writer exchange love letters. She saves his letters religiously, and she tells him: Save my letters, too. He writes back: I have to burn your letters because my present girlfriend might come across them and get upset, but you'll always be my one and only true love, you know that, you and I are the same person. Forty years later, the male writer dies, the female writer publishes the love letters he had sent her and declares to

70

the world: Look how truly he loved me, he said so on every page – I, too, in the incinerated letters, said I loved him truly . . .

The letter O burned out. The letters gone up in smoke. Alix gone, too, and then the spring arriving. The insufferable spring. Bird-song, bursts of laughter, music floating freely in the air. Sounds reached my ears through a glass box: muted, stifled, dissolved. People looked deformed and fuzzy, infinitely far away. I was in constant fear of breaking the glass box, lacerating my hands on the shards. But at the same time the box was my own personalised vehicle, four sheets of glass that surrounded me wherever I went: I was protected but cut off. Definitively cut off.

'And that's when your problem with razors and knives began?'

'No, before. Only before, I could keep it under control.'

'Whereas in the glass box?'

'It was there to prevent me from making any rash gestures. Everything in slow motion. Or else . . .'

'Hence your incapacity to drive a car.'

'Out of the question. Everything in slow motion . . . Even public transport was forbidden.'

'Because you'd run the risk of being touched?'

'Of breaking the glass.'

'So you went everywhere on foot?'

'On foot. If at all.'

There's a bus that leaves from the University and goes towards the city centre, Omaya gets on but the bus's number changes en route, it drives through unfamiliar neighbourhoods swarming with lugubrious crowds of people, it passes in front of a station and Omaya jumps off, she manages to get her bearings on a map of the city

71

but then takes the wrong train, it's not a local but an express train and it won't stop until it gets to the suburbs . . . When she finally reaches the end of the line, Omaya tries to change platforms but the stairways are cut off by men working, she decides to cross the tracks though she's vaguely aware the rails are electrified, she treads carefully on the ground in between them, then she hears the train . . . Toot, toot! She wakes up, she mustn't fall asleep, all it would take is a moment's distraction and I'd be hopelessly lost, irrevocably separated from my family, my friends, everything and everyone I know, I'd wander through the infinite complexity of the city, getting on buses at random and asking whether by any chance they're headed for a destination whose name I might recognise, but they're invariably headed for the outskirts and never for the city centre, and I end up . . . No, I don't end up, it never ends, it just keeps starting all over again, every single time they have to take it from the top . . .

'You're all by yourself? Can we buy you a drink? What are you doing out in this dreadful weather in such an unsavoury neighbourhood?'

'I've just left the Castle, I wanted to go to the city centre.'

'It's pretty late, you know, the buses have stopped running.'

'Yes, I know. I was thinking I'd call a friend and ask her to come and pick me up . . .'

'We could drive you over to her place, if you like.'

'That's nice of you – but no, thanks. Don't put yourselves out.'

The car takes off, goes through a red light and takes a right turn. We're going unthinkably fast. Right turn.

Another red light ignored – don't worry. There's no one in the street at this time of night. Accelerator. Stop sign, a pedestrian crossing. The brakes screech. An old lady. I almost got her. What the fuck's she doing out so late at night? Left turn. The woman in white squeezed in between two men in black. Her left arm next to a right arm. Her right arm next to a left arm. The car swerves. Contact. The head spins. In front of us: two headlights rendered ghostlike by the rain. Beep, beep! *Achtung!* You have nothing to fear. I know how to drive. What about you, do you know how to drive? I know this neighbourhood like the back of my hand. Right turn. You see? That's the coffee-shop there.

The coffee-shop is deserted. They have the keys. The buses aren't running any more. It's too late. The neon lights come on.

Anastasia, I can't do it. I know I have to, but I can't. Even with you sitting beside me on the bench. Even with all your knowledge to support me. How do you manange to be so solid, to keep all those words and phrases, laws and precedents in your head at the same time? I know I can count on you, it's Omaya that I'm afraid might walk out on me . . .

Anastasia knows how to get around in the world. She has knowledge, money and convictions. She'll come by taxi. So will the other lawyer. Two women dressed in black, each in her own taxi and each in her own right. They know their rights. A hand waved in the air: Taxi! pronounced in an imperious tone of voice. And the taxi is there, at their disposal. They get into the back seat, princesses giving orders to their coachmen, and they are obeyed. The drivers go exactly where they tell them to go. They have money in their handbags, and it's money they've earned themselves. What else is in the bags? Pens and penal codes, notebooks and circulars, certainly no make-up. Their faces are frankness incarnate. The un- varnished truth. Full stop. That is all.

When Lorna wrote, Full stop: that is all, she meant precisely that. She was capable of spending the whole morning sitting up in bed, a pen in her hand, a notebook on her drawn-up knees, lost in the contemplation of a tiny imperfection on the page. For her, a full stop was *all*: it filled her whole horizon, it held secrets she strove tirelessly to decipher. As soon as she'd written a single word, she regretted having murdered all the other words with which she might have begun her poem. That's why her poems were so short: she wanted to murder as few words as possible.

She was afraid of everything. In the beginning, she refused to speak to me or even look at me. But once she'd seen that I had no intention of invading her privacy, that I respected her immobility and her muteness, she made an attempt to find out who I was. At first she contented herself with watching me out of the corner of her eye, on the sly, when she thought I was asleep. Later, she would come and sit on the edge of the bed where I was smoking, and scrutinise me anxiously. I let her. So long as people didn't touch me, I didn't care what they did. She would whisper:

'You're Omaya?'
'Yes.'
'I see . . .'
After a long pause, she'd resume:
'You're Omaya? One single person?'
'That's right. All of me is Omaya, all of Omaya is me.'
'Then why don't your eyes agree with your mouth?'

'Nothing agrees with anything.'

Lorna could never manage to study my whole face at the same time. Her eyes would be riveted, now at the top and now at the bottom. She was sure the respective messages were contradictory, and despite all her efforts, she simply couldn't reconcile them.

'Never mind, Lorna.'

'Everyone.'

'What do you mean, everyone?'

'Never mind Lorna, everyone.'

People without keys often feel sorry for themselves. I'm sixty-five, almost ready to kick the bucket. That's why they're incapable of feeling sorry for others. Same with me. I'd settle back behind my smokescreen and leave her silent and alone on the other side.

The inevitable horde of youths. The air in the car is jostled by their bickering voices. Girls in groups are different, but no less despicable, they giggle. They talk in whispers, tickling one another's ears, and then start squealing louder and louder, their piercing artificial laughs cause every vertebra in the spine to grate. But these are bellowing, arrogant, hollow voices.

'You think skiing's the hardest sport? Skiing's nothing, all you've got to do is let yourself slide.'

'Yeah, but if you make the least mistake you can be dead the next second.'

'Yeah but still, it's not hard at all, he's right, it's not tiring. I think wrestling's the hardest.'

'Come on! Wrestling's a sham, everyone knows that. Motor racing's a lot more dangerous. A lot more people end up in the morgue after motor racing than wrestling.'

'My dad plays tennis every Sunday, it's a hell of a lot

harder than it looks. By the end of a match he's totally whacked.'

'Then your dad must be a weakling. For my dad, playing tennis is about as tiring as shaving.'

'It all depends on what you mean by hard, whether you mean difficult, or dangerous, or tiring. My dad's been teaching me to play chess recently and, let me tell you, it's hard in the sense of difficult, compared to any other sport –'

'Chess isn't a sport, we were talking about sports!'

'Yeah, but there are lots of sports where you've got to be intelligent, too, like –'

'If chess isn't a sport, how come they have chess in the Olympic Games? Eh? Can you tell me that?'

'Team sports are hard as hell, too – nobody's even mentioned them. In football you can get squashed like a flea.'

'What about mountain-climbing? Have you ever tried scrambling up a vertical cliff on a rope? With the crevice waiting for you down below, its jaws wide open? I did that last summer . . .'

'Stop bragging. It's no more dangerous than being a circus acrobat.'

'Like hell! Acrobats have nets underneath.'

'Not always. I saw one fall once, and he snuffed it.'

'When was that?'

'Oh, a long time ago . . .'

'You liar, you're just making it up. You were so ugly your mother didn't even want to take you to the circus, she was afraid they'd mistake you for a clown.'

'Your mother's the one who looks like a clown.'

'What was that?'

'He didn't say anything, he just sneezed, that's all, ignore him, he's nothing but a snotty little brat.'

'Bless you, then.'

'Is this our stop?'

'Listen to him, he claims to have travelled to the four corners of the earth and he can't find his way round the underground. Not even with a map in front of his face. Take a look at the map, that'll keep you busy till the next stop, and then you can take the teacher's hand like a good little boy so you won't get lost.'

'Shut it, will you?'

Stop it! If only they'd stop, just for a few seconds, so I could get hold of myself. But they're talking at top speed, interrupting each other, taking off on a word, an association, and I can't follow them, or not follow them, their words surround me, drug me, make me dizzy. All I had was one drink, whereas they've been drinking for hours, so why is my head spinning like this? Oh my God, yes, it must be those flowers intoxicating me, I forgot this morning's flowers and I had a drink . . .

The personalised tray, every morning at breakfast. A painter's palette. Pastel pills. Pink, white, yellow, pale green, pale blue: a bouquet for Omaya. The loveliest ones have names ending in *-ium* or in *-ia*. Who sent me this magnificent bouquet? Nasturtium, wisteria. Geranium, astromeria. And spurge. And the pink roses that bloom so quickly, the pink roses that explode, their petals floating softly down and down . . . It's a wedding, people are throwing handfuls of rose petals at the head of the bride, it's a wedding, people are throwing handfuls of rice at the head of the bride, it's a wedding, people are throwing stones at the head of the bride, she cheated on her husband, she must die, I'll never cheat on you with anyone but my illness, and now it's come to that, Alix, I love my illness more than you, at least it keeps me company, at least it stays with me all the time, whereas you, you value your independence, you come and go as you please, you never wanted us to live together completely and now it is too late, your rival has moved in with me, and thanks to her I receive multi-coloured flowers every morning, all I have to do is swallow them and wait for the sweet explosion of the petals: Ah! how heavenly it is.

A woman writer died young, and towards the end of her illness, before being gagged once and for all, she cried out: The rose! ROSE WITH VIOLET HEART – and all the men around her were delighted, it was indeed appropriate that this woman should die, she who had had such a profound understanding of the connection – VIOLATED HEART DARES TO KILL – between love and death. As for them, they lived on for many years, and spent those years writing and preaching love and deaths and brandishing as proof the death and love of this young woman who, even younger, had lived with a man who put a dog collar around her throat – OPEN THROAT SHALL BE LAW – kept her on a leash and fed her sandwiches buttered with his shit . . .

I'm not hungry, I'll never be hungry again, and dogs are totally out of place here, you're not supposed to bring them into the underground, even a poodle in a wicker basket isn't allowed, you never know, the poodle might leap out of its basket and bite you and give you rabies. I'm sure her Honour has a poodle, she buys him very expensive hand-knitted angora sweaters, she walked him this morning as she does every morning, berating him the way a mother berates her child in the pastry-shop, don't touch this, don't touch that, in an exasperated tone of voice. The dog has grown mean over the years, it yelps from morning to night, it sinks its pointed teeth into the ankles of passers-by, only there are virtually no passers-by since her Honour lives in an isolated mansion far away from the city, a mansion surrounded by high walls on which she's scattered broken glass to protect herself from robbers, she never walks her poodle outside the walls, she forces it to do its business under the bushes, right here and not an inch away, right now and not a second later. The days she has to come into the city to judge, she leaves the dog tied up in the garden for twelve hours on end. She drives her car to the station, buys a first-class ticket: her Honour will come by train.

Day is breaking, she's alone in her compartment, she's looking out the window but sees nothing of the country-side, she sees only her own reflection, ever since childhood she's observed herself like this in the window pane every time she takes a train, but with less and less enjoyment, today she strives to recognise in her features something of the adolescent she used to be, the smooth skin, the full lips, the eyes she loved more than anything in the world, she would gaze deeply into her own eyes and tell herself that no man would ever be able to resist that, now she sees two permanent furrows between the eyebrows, hollowed out by constant frowning, it's unfair that years of work should mark one thus, leaving their indelible imprint, it's unfair, it's unfair, young women these days don't know what real work means, we cleared the way for them by the sweat of our brows, we had to be strong, tenacious, stubborn, and we were, and now they whimper like little babies, they whine and complain about how hard life is. They've never had to face hunger or hardship, that's why they're so flabby-minded and spoiled, they're rotten to the core, they think that freedom means taking drugs, drinking, dancing, making love at random and nipping in the bud whatever children might result, they have no sense of discipline or hierarchy or rectitude.

Raise your right leg: one, two, three, four. Lower your leg: one, two, three, four. Stay with the beat. The small of your back should be flattened against the floor. Now your left leg. Raise: one, two, three, four. Lower: one, two, three, four. Bring yourselves to a sitting position. Not just any old way, Omaya. *Gracefully*. Even transitional movements should be elegant. Do it again. Keep your heels on the floor, tighten your abdominal muscles, and now lift your head off the ground, yes, and now your neck, now your backbone, one vertebra at a time – there, that's better. Now, everyone: spread your legs and grasp your left foot with both hands, without bending your knees. Lean forward until your forehead is resting on your knee. Remain in that position. Exhale. Inhale. Exhale. Inhale.

Their gasps.
'You hold her arms. I'll get her legs.'

The gym classes are because of my clumsiness. Cybele complains that I'm always making wild gestures: bumping into furniture, knocking over glasses . . . You must have grown too fast, she says, you haven't got used to your new body yet – your young woman's body – it's important to take good care of the body because it's the haven of the mind. Your mind's okay, she says, school will help to make it strong and supple, but your body should learn some kind of discipline, too – ballet, for example, only she despises ballerinas, she says their tiny heads are filled with marshmallow – so what about gymnastics, now there's a hearty, healthy discipline, she herself does ten minutes of yoga every morning before getting dressed, before gathering her lustrous flowing hair into a chignon, I watch her, her forehead is resting on her knee, her hair is radiating all around like sunlight, she's so beautiful . . .

'But you formerly asserted that Cybele attributed Omaya's clumsiness to the excessive length of her fringe.'

'I'm going to shave my head. That way you won't have to cut my hair any more.'

She burst out laughing, she didn't believe me. I grabbed the scissors. The razor. The razor-blade starts hacking away. Before making the incision, it is advisable to shave the patient's head completely. A matter of hygiene. At the base of the skull, the scar goes from one ear to the other like a huge, idiotic grin. Or is it on the forehead?

Omaya is incapable of resting her forehead on her knee. She looks at her feet, her tights have holes in them, the big toe as usual, these tights are almost new, they can't be mended because they're made of some synthetic stuff instead of wool, I'm the only one who comes here every week with holes in my tights, holes taunt me and torment me. If ever, in a moment of expansiveness, I put my hands behind my neck and stretch, someone will point out that right there, under my arm, there's a rip in my sweater . . . Or else there'll be a thread dangling from the hem of my skirt, or a button missing from my jersey, to say nothing of laddered stockings, tangled necklaces, frayed cuffs, broken heels, and how do the other girls manage to be so impeccable, their mothers must help them with their clothes before they leave for school, Cybele never thinks about that sort of thing, she is impeccable by nature, just as bright and clean as the machines with which she spends the better part of her time, how does she expect me to become an actress if I always look untidy, you can't show up for auditions dressed the way I am, I'd like to start again from scratch, buy myself a whole new wardrobe, clothes are always so lovely when you see them in the store, when I try them on for the first time in the dressing-room they're even lovelier and they communicate their loveliness to me, I look at myself enchanted, but once the clothes are paid for they gradually deteriorate, they grow more and more frumpy and faded, as though *I* were now communicating my invisible taints to *them* . . . Contamination! After a few months they look just like me and I despise them, I can't face myself in the mirror. What I like best is borrowing the clothes of a Friend, wearing another woman's dress or scarf or blouse for a single evening, that way I can put on her personality at the same time and it makes me feel so free, I have the right to talk and eat as I imagine she would do. Alix didn't like lending me her clothes, she never wanted to hang them up in the wardrobe next to mine, all she brought was a suitcase containing a few possessions, and even that she hid under the bed and asked me not to touch . . . Contamination! What I like best are theatre costumes, they belong neither to me nor to anyone else, they belong to an imaginary woman, she can't resent me spoiling her things, she lends me her gestures, her thoughts, her memories, she caresses me inside and out, I can borrow anything I want from her and she never feels dispossessed, she accepts me, we live completely together, I look at her in the mirror, I smile at her and she smiles back, she prompts me whenever I forget my lines, she keeps my mind and body in order. She is many. I have adored every woman I've ever played . . .

82

Perhaps even more than the Friends.

'And what is it you're playing right at this moment?'

'I'm playing Sincerity, the most difficult role ever.'

'You're not entirely convincing.'

'That's because I've never met Sincerity. Her script hasn't been written yet.'

'She's just play-acting. Stop screaming or we'll give you something to scream about.'

'The world, despite what some may claim, is not a stage. Life is more than role-playing.'

'As soon as I stop acting, I am no one. I'm nothing but pure fear.'

Giant black words broken by creases – FEAR – HUSBAND – SHE CONSENTS – BY HER BOSS! The woman reading them is young, she works in an office, her fingernails are cut short for the IBM but freshly painted, she's made her face up carefully this morning, like every morning, every woman, look at them, every single one, every one but Omaya, they've got up early so as to work over their carcasses, plucking, colouring, discolouring, smearing on, cutting off, slitting their throats, sealing their leaks, trying to prevent their liquids from oozing out, covering up their fetid odours with heady perfumes, but Omaya can smell them, despite the toilet water the Cologne water the rose water, she can smell the nauseating stenches seeping from their armpits and their crotches, mounting insistently, irrepressibly, denouncing these women for what they really are: putrefying flesh.

This particular one is wearing glasses but she hopes a man will notice, behind the picture windows, her eyelids which were decorated with smokey-blue the minute she got up at six. Immediately her eyes had opened, they were daubed with seductiveness for the hours to come – in hopes that, after the solitary breakfast gulped down in the kitchen, after the blandness of the underground spiced up with salacious true stories, after the first hour spent belabouring the lettered keys, her head still buzzing with FEAR – HUSBAND – SHE CONSENTS – BY HER BOSS – when she goes to get a cup of coffee from the machine, or else during her lunch-hour in the cafeteria, a man will notice that her eyelids, instead of being stupidly natural-white, are smokey-blue, and he'll appreciate the subtle contrast between the hue of the lids and that of the irises underneath, and be amazed by such a striking proof of good taste in a place where one would least expect it, and one thing leading to another, this woman would no longer gulp down solitary breakfasts. Everywhere I look it's the same thing: the phoney pearls on hairy old ears, the spots of shocking pink on ashen cheeks, the tubes of mascara in the handbags of the Wives, and all of them are telling themselves that, one thing leading to another . . .

'When did you stop paying attention to your femininity?'

'No more mirrors . . . except at the Theatre.'

'At the theatre, that is, when the face you see is no longer your own but that of another woman, your character?'

'Make-up is no longer allowed, except for the people who borrow my body to play the woman.'

'In other words, offstage, you yourself are not a woman? What are you, then?'

. . .

'How did you come to deserve this punishment?'

'Cybele punished me because I stole her lipstick.'

'Yes?'

'Alix punished me because I looked at myself in the mirror for years and years.'

'So it's always other people who punish you, is that right?'

Alix, oh Alix, I don't want to lose you, I love you, I love only you, but Saroyan, being in bed with Saroyan, for the first time it's nothing like a punishment – yes, it is possible, I beg of you, listen to me, don't interrupt me, don't make that face, listen – he enters me and then he doesn't move, he's there and I can feel him and I arch my body against his, he desires my desire, he doesn't try to stop me, pin me down, stifle me, he wants me alive and this is the first time that a man, you can't be angry with me for feeling this way, you can't, you want me alive too, you know you're the one I love but let me hold on to this, I beg of you, you must understand how much it reassures me . . .

And, one thing leading to another, Omaya was left to gulp her breakfast down alone, or else to gulp down nothing at all, or else to gulp down only the bouquet of flowers and leave her breakfast on the tray, a cup of lukewarm water with a packet of powdered coffee, a packet of powdered sugar, a packet of powdered milk, a roll, a pat of butter, a portion of jam. One thing leading to another. I've lost the thread.

'Could you give us the exact meaning of the following sayings: to lose the thread, to lose one's head, to wash one's dirty linen in public, he who hesitates is lost, curiosity killed the cat, there's no smoke without fire? Please have the courtesy to answer as clearly and as concisely as possible. Ready? Go. Number one. What does the expression to lose the thread mean?'

'It means that when you're sewing, you must never let the thread of your thoughts escape you, you must try to concentrate, doing something with your hands is excellent for concentration, here, for example, the women all sit together knitting in the same room, they talk as they knit and their chatter draws me out of my concentric circle, I lose the thread, the needles pierce my palms, I have stigmata . . . No, it's not my palms, it's my wrists, or else the insides of my elbows, the needle thrusts beneath the skin and ejects its liquid, this will calm you down, this will keep you quiet, this will stop your screaming.'

'That's fine. Now, look at these ink blots: what do they remind you of?'

'A shipwreck, or an owl swooping down on a rabbit – your examinations are too easy, I know the answers before I've even heard the questions, I'm used to it after living with Cybele, you won't catch me with mere ink blots.'

'What about if we put the ink *into* the needle? And if the needle thrusts beneath the skin and ejects its liquid – what would you call that?'

'A tattoo. Or if you prefer: a sentimental novel.'

'That's fine. Now, try to explain this. Your Honour, I'm going to ask you to hold the point of this needle between your thumb and index finger. Now, I'll attempt to slip this thread through the eye of the needle, and I'd like you to do everything you can to prevent me. One, two, three . . . missed. One, two, three . . . missed again. There, you see? It's impossible: if the needle moves, the thread is impotent. The demonstration is irrefutable. The proof is positive.'

If you hold the thread in your left hand, it won't get

tangled when you pull the needle through with your right.
Always work from left to right, with the light coming over
your left shoulder so that the shadow of your right hand
won't be projected onto the part of the hem you're sewing.
The pattern formed by the thread is a series of tiny Xs:
XXXXXXXXXXX, just like when you correct typing errors,
only in this case correction is not possible, it has to be
perfect the first time round, your needle should never pick
up more than a single thread at a time, if the needle goes
through the cloth it will be visible from the other side and
everyone will know you've hemmed your dress, instead of
thinking it was born that way, smooth and impeccable,
always keep in mind that the only proper sewing job is an
invisible one. If, due to a moment's distraction, you
should allow the needle to go through the cloth, to pierce
the membrane, the damage would be irreparable. We
don't know how to fix that kind of tear nowadays, all
attempts to remedy the situation would be doomed to
failure, the dress would be unsellable, no man would ever
admire it, always keep in mind that young women should
remain smooth and impeccable, your very life may
depend on it.

Stop it! Stop veering off in all directions, this is no time to
lose the thread, I have to concentrate . . . But I'm not
allowed in the Concentration room any more, its play-
school colours and atmosphere are forbidden to me. I
don't care . . . Omaya found it intolerable, that parody of
the city within the Castle . . . The keyless women would
gather there to learn to concentrate, for example they'd be
filling up little bags with multi-coloured sweets, all of
their little fingers flying, all of their little heads bent over,
all of them mimicking factory workers with grotesque
seriousness, and the women with keys would clap their

hands: Congratulations! You've filled up twenty-six little bags of sweets today! And the keyless women would blush with pleasure and stammer thank you when, at the end of the month, they received their pathetic wages. They could either squander this money by going to the coffee-shop every day and ordering a cup of real coffee, or else save it up and buy themselves a new blouse for the mixed ball at the end of December, a ball which would last from two until five in the afternoon, at which time the dining-hall would have to be cleared for the evening meal. Balls are a hearty, healthy discipline, they draw you out of yourself and help you meet other people. And so the women in the Concentration room worked day after day and dreamed about their romances to come, just as the young girls of yesteryear embroidered their trousseaus and dreamed about Prince Charming, you mustn't dream, all it would take is a moment's distraction for the needle to pierce the membrane, they would prick their fingers and fall asleep for a hundred years . . . Then one day Omaya, unable to live in the fairy-tale any longer, plunges her hands into the box full of multi-coloured sweets, tosses a shower of confetti at the heads of the brides, a hail of stones at the heads of the brides: Rejoice! Shed tears of multi-coloured ecstasy! Sweetness should not be shut up in little bags, it should spurt forth and splash onto the walls . . .

'And then what happened?'

'*Achtung!* Alarm on every face. And shortly afterwards: the needle.'

'They tell me you made a scene the other day . . . They had to step in to calm you down.'

'It's because it gets too calm around here sometimes.'

'But you can leave any time you want, Omaya. Why do

you stay here, if you find it too calm?'

. . .

'Seriously, darling . . . I must admit this last episode worried me a little. For the first time, I wondered whether . . .'

'I just wanted to celebrate. It was like confetti.'

'My God . . . You sound exactly like your father.'

'Really? You mean he used to enjoy splattering gaudy sweetness, too?'

'Omaya, stop it! Why do you talk like that? It frightens me . . . We're losing the track . . .'

'Yes, Cybele. Losing the track. How well you put it.'

Stay on the track. Never wander from the straight and narrow. Do not follow the Owl, who strays too far from the beaten track. If you agree to accompany him in his night walks in the forest, you must accept the consequences. The thorn piercing your sole and entering your heel. The throbbing pain: a stroke of lightning going up instead of down, setting the brain ablaze. Omaya screams. The Owl stops and turns: What is it? Omaya has collapsed at the foot of a tree. The thorn has disappeared beneath the surface of the skin, setting off pulsations, incandescent waves. The heel has already started to swell.

'This will just take a minute, pet.'

The Owl is heating water on a burner of the kitchen stove. He is watching me. He sees Omaya's hands gripping the edge of her chair, he sees her contorted lips. He comes back towards me with a basin full of water. The water is boiling hot.

'You're going to have to stick your foot in and hold it there. Do it – for me. It'll hurt, but it's for your own good. Otherwise, I'll never be able to remove the thorn. Do you trust me? Okay, Omaya. It's all right, pet.'

The train has stopped. What's wrong? We're in between stations and we've stopped moving, the lights have dimmed, the tension is rising, the other passengers have stopped talking . . . Each of them is silently wondering: a bomb on the tracks? A suicide? The driver suddenly taken ill? The carriage is packed – as long as we were moving the crowding was bearable, now it isn't, you can see the anxiety in everybody's eyes . . . No, only in Omaya's, the other passengers are merely impatient, they're looking at their watches, tapping their feet, and sighing in exasperation. That's the normal way to react. There isn't the least danger, nothing is wrong, the train will start up again any moment now . . .

'Today, improvisation: Omaya and Saroyan. Omaya, you are a young woman, you're waiting for the underground late at night, you're alone on the platform, it's past midnight, the train doesn't come, a young man does come, however – that's you, Saroyan, you notice this woman standing at the far end of the platform, you approach her, what will happen next, will you speak to one another, will you hit one another, it's up to you to decide on the basis of the inner truth of your characters. Go ahead.'

The platform is filthy. Omaya creates the filth, she calls it forth around her, she brings debris and litter and the smell of urine into existence, her mind replays the evening the young woman has just lived through, an evening filled with greasy phrases, she feels her body going numb with fatigue and despondency. Little by little, she invokes the tunnel, the long and silent hole of blackness, she listens with all her might but not a sound emerges from the chasm, she looks with all her might but not a glimmer of light breaks through, the tunnel's darkness and silence seem intrinsic and definitive, I've spent my whole life waiting for the train, scrutinising tunnels that nothing ever comes to fill, it's inconceivable that such an emptiness could give birth to my salvation: the train that would take me closer to home and to oblivion.

Omaya is not waiting, she is hovering. The tunnel is waiting passively to be filled up by the train, but Omaya is working actively to make it appear, she's wishing for it with all her might, she hurls her will into the void and watches it plummet to the ground, her will crashes in the dark without a sound . . . And then suddenly, behind her, above her: a man.

'Excuse me . . . Have you been waiting long?'

She spins around, without the least hesitation, she throws herself at the stranger and shoves him with all her might onto the tracks, she knows it will work, in Westerns all you have to do is tie someone to the tracks and the train appears as if by magic, now it's sure to come, there's not the slightest doubt . . . And Saroyan on the floor gasping for breath, and the other actors and the director aghast, and Omaya triumphant and so proud to have dared at last, to have defended herself at last . . . No, she's made a mistake, she's over-reacted, her actor's instinct has led her astray, and that is serious. It's very serious if even at the Theatre she starts to lose her head.

'Are you ready? What is the meaning of the expression to lose one's head? Every second of hesitation will cost you one point.'

'To lose one's head, that means that when you're riding a bicycle and you come to the top of a hill, the descent is very steep and the wheels start turning faster and faster, your head goes flying off into the air and you can't control the machine, you can't restrain yourself, you can't be held responsible, it isn't your fault if you run over people that get in your way, there's nothing you can do about it, once you've started you have to go all the way.'

'Not bad. Passable.'

'Not bad. She's not bad at all.'

'Look, I've done what you asked me to do, now I'm going to put my clothes back on. It's cold in here and I'm not feeling well. All right?'

'Is that all right? What do you say? Is it all right with us if she puts her clothes back on?'

'It's not all right with me.'

'Me, neither.'

'Me, neither.'

'Me, neither. What do you say? Shall we take a vote?'

'Ha ha.'

'Let's take a vote!'

'You gave me your word of honour, you told me that if I . . .'

'We've changed our minds, love. Rotten luck.'

'Let me go, please. Please let me go.'

'She doesn't seem to understand what I just told her. Wasn't it clear?'

'Sounded clear enough to me, ha ha.'

'Maybe we should teach her to pay attention when grown-ups speak to her?'

Once you've started you have to go all the way. Once you've taken the car and driven into the middle of a tunnel with the engine overheating, you have no choice, you must live through the event from beginning to end. Once you've gone onstage for the first act, you can't change your mind halfway through, you're obliged to go back for the second and the third. Once you've started feeling the contractions, you can't do anything about it, the whole thing has to unfold until there's been a birth or a death, even if it entails scenes of butchery, your feet in stirrups, your arms tied down by leather straps, your shrieking body drawn and quartered by the pain.

A keyless woman is seized by the bird of panic, she starts running down the corridors and banging her head against the walls, they tie her down to her bed with heavy leather straps, her body heaves upwards, ecstatically arched to receive the needle . . .

A woman of the Wild West is kidnapped by outlaws, they tear off her flowery hat and frilly dress, she stands there trembling in her button-boots, they tear off her lace pantaloons and lace bodice, they cram her lace hankie into her mouth, they contemplate her shame and help-lessness with satisfaction, they tie her to the railway tracks with heavy cords, this invariably causes the train to appear, the woman faints and is left for dead, but just then – exactly a hundred years later – Prince Charming comes galloping to the rescue . . .

And Omaya drawn and quartered, her head her hands her feet tied down by straps of flesh, her mouth stopped up with a gag of flesh, once it has started it has to go all the way, she waits a hundred years and more, she can wait for ever, no one will come, she is unrescuable, it will be the month of December for ever, it will be cold for ever, she'll be there for ever feeling the train running over her body, its wheels as sharp as knives, sawing at her bones like electric saws spinning unthinkably fast, each of them digging its separate groove, that's what happens when people lose their heads . . .

'But *what* actually happened, that evening? When it comes down to it, they neither kidnapped you nor removed your clothes by force. You got undressed yourself, by your own admission. What happened was, essentially, nothing at all.'

Essentially nothing. Nothing is the very essence of a tunnel. Tunnels are empty by definition. I must force myself to concentrate on the walls and put a halt to these words. Empty out my mind, as Saroyan would say. Stop turning the whole thing over, or I'll drown myself in the flood of words. But nothing can stop my train of thought – one of Lorna's poems? – nothing, not even sleep, sleeping's worse than waking. You have insomnia because you're afraid of what your dreams might reveal. Yes, so flowers to sleep a dreamless sleep, and more flowers to live a dreamless life . . . Saroyan tells me: meditation is better than medication, sit in the lotus position, empty out your mind, breathe deeply, let me give you a massage . . . DON'T TOUCH ME!

In one hour it will have started and I'm going to have to convince them I have the keys, this is not the time to misplace them again, Omaya, listen . . . In the little restaurant next to the Theatre, I would always sit next to a table at which two people were already talking, it would sometimes give me ideas for my characters, most often they'd be men in blue who worked at the factory nearby and who'd come in for a quick lunch, they'd be discussing things that had nothing to do with the play but I'd catch a sentence in mid-air, sometimes only a word – tight, chalky, flattened – and it would be like a piece of advice for the performance, I'd be able to use it, so listen . . .

'Great bloke. Right on target. Not the preening type. Not finical.'

'Couldn't agree with you more.'

'He introduced me to his fiancée last week.'

'She's ill, naturally?'

'Dying.'

'The eye of God?'

'Right in the mouth. Right on target.'

'You don't say! He must be rather intrigued by it all.'

'Exactly. You have to know what you can count on.'

'And he knows, does he?'

'Trustworthy. Never misses a beat.'

'I thought so. If only I had his gall, his gallantry.'

'Yes. We're only human, aren't we?'

'Just the same, it *is* rather too bad. It's raining cats and dogs.'

'The better to bite you with, old man.'

'Yeah. It's almost funny, when you come to think about it.'

Don't listen, that's not it, that's not it, those are Omaya's own words, don't pay the least attention, she'll get over it, I beseech you, don't desert her, listen, I'll make an effort to be more clear . . .

'Why can't you speak clearly, instead of waving your arms around and expressing yourself in onomatopoeia? You look like a comic strip! What is language for, in your opinion?'

'Omaya, your teacher says . . .'

'I know, I know.'

'But why, darling? Why do you refuse to talk in class these days?'

'It's not that I refuse to talk, it's just that words are not enough. They're in black and white, they look so bleak all by themselves, so I feel like adding a bit of colour.'

'Oh! . . . that's rather pretty. But it isn't true that words are in black and white. The word rose, for example – what colour is it?'

'The letters are black with white space around them. The sounds are black with white air around them.'

'Not at all! What's the use of writing poetry, if it isn't to paint a beautiful picture using the whole phonetic palette?'

'I never said writing poetry was any use.'

'Listen, darling . . . The brain we passed down to you is divided into two parts, one verbal and the other emotional, there's no reason to favour one above the other, it's unfair, it's almost as if you preferred your father to your mother, the right hemisphere to the left, it's unthinkable!'

She didn't say that, I've gone off the track again, Cybele has never talked to me that way, more lies, do you swear to speak without hatred or fear, to tell the whole truth and nothing but the truth, I swear that if I knew how other people do it, I'd do the same, but all of you have learned your lines by heart, whereas I haven't a single line at my disposal, millions of books have been written about this but what happened to Omaya has never been touched by words, as soon as words come near it they're repelled, the way a negative magnet is repelled by a negative magnet, the Owl taught me that, two magnets with the same charge can never come together, the negative words won't stick to the negative thing, they bounce off and start to whirl around, colliding with one another, they refuse to align themselves politely into sentences, with all the words in the world I could never make you feel so much as the first slap in the face, the shock of that, the outrage of that, the tears that spring to the eyes, the cheek that stings, and then their fingers encircling Omaya's wrists like hand-cuffs, the muscles of their arms like a vice, their touch so stunning that it makes my own muscles useless, my own strength absurd, and then the coarse grain of their skin in close-up, and the sourness of their breath, their sweat, all their juices, for you these are nothing but words and you won't understand a thing, because THEY, THEY'RE the ones who have the keys to the mystery, and without the keys all I can do is keep repeating myself and going around in circles and getting lost in the maze of the Castle.

'Why the Castle?'

'Here, my little wife, take these keys, the keys to every door in my Castle, but you must never ever use the smallest one, it unlocks the door to the cupboard at the far end of the hall, I'm giving it to you, but don't go into the secret cupboard, here is the key, there is the door, don't open it, don't try to find out what is inside, I'm giving you the key so that you shall never use it, is that quite clear?'

'If I understand correctly, you have the key, but you're not allowed to use it?'

'No – not the key to the mystery. But what is in the cupboard is not a mystery. It's common knowledge.'

'What?'

. . .

'Tell me. What is it?'

. . .

'It's just a fairy-tale, Omaya.'

'So are the newspapers and the radio and the history books, so many fairy-tales in which blue and white and black beards, crowned and cowled heads, reveal the

97

sinister contents of their secret cupboards: you turn the page, you open the door, and the competition begins: how many of them are there? How many rabbits hanging from nails, dangling upside-down? Five? Ten? Twenty? Fifty? Will the contemporary Lords be able to beat the record of their ancestors?'

'Why the Lords?'

'Because Lords can go anywhere they like, they know where they're going and how to get there, they have all the keys, they open all the doors – After you! – inserting their keys without even looking, thrusting them into car doors, ignitions and boots, the keys never get stuck or mislaid, they're like an appendage of the body, always ready for action, the Lords use them automatically, they consider them from a purely utilitarian point of view, as a means to an end.'

'And the end? What is the end?'

'Everyone knows the ending. It's no surprise.'

'Why did you disobey me? Why did you open the door to the secret cupboard?'

'I beg your pardon . . . I didn't quite catch the question.'

'Why were you rummaging around in the medicine cabinet?'

'I was looking for some aspirin, I had a headache.'

'What did you take?'

'Just aspirin.'

'There wasn't any aspirin. What pills did you take?'

'Don't touch me! Please . . . What was it you asked me?'

'We can hardly hear you, young lady. Couldn't you at least make an effort to speak audibly? Silence in the court. The Prosecution has asked you for an explanation of your suicide attempt.'

'The Prosecution?'

The Friends start singing. Their voices are coloured ribbons floating gently in the air, in tones of dusky rose, violet and deep purple which flout the sombre bearings of the judge, the lawyers, the policemen; twining themselves maliciously in their hair; insinuating themselves into their ears; the Friends are holding hands and swaying to and fro, soothing Omaya with their mellow harmonies. The gavel slices through the air and strikes, the voices are extinguished, the words in black and white start up again.

'Silence in the court. Members of the public are warned that if this kind of disturbance is repeated, I will order the courtroom to be cleared immediately, and the remainder of the proceedings to be held *in camera*. Now, if the Prosecution would be so kind as to repeat her question . . .'

'What were the main reasons behind your attempt to end your life?'

'Saroyan had taken me to listen to some ancient music in a church. The concert was being given by a children's choir from a nearby summer camp. The music was pure and joyful, the children's mouths were open wide, as round as Os, their voices soared together in perfect harmony, no voice could possibly have deviated from its vibrant line of notes, not one could possibly have faltered, the children's voices held each other up and their eyes glittered with ardent conviction . . .'

'Go on . . .'

'But gradually . . . it began to dawn on me why the children were pouring their bodies and souls into the music like that. It was because . . .'

'Yes?'

'Because they were . . . condemned.'

'Could you clarify that term for us, please?'

'The summer camp was a concentration camp, they were being forced to concentrate, compelled to sing, if they sang off-key they'd be gunned down on the spot, the joyful music was false, an abominable sham, its only purpose was to decorate the horror, their mouths were round with fear, their eyes were glittering with tears, I started . . .'

'Go on.'

'. . . to cry myself, and Saroyan squeezed my hand as if to say, I know what you're feeling, it's so beautiful, and then . . .'

'And then?'

'. . . afterwards, once we'd left the church, I couldn't tell him. He was so kind, so trusting, I felt ashamed.'

'So you knew quite well that your vision did not correspond to reality?'

'We're getting off the track again, your Honour. What connection could there possibly be between this event in my client's life, which dates from a rather distant past, and the facts we are here today to ascertain?'

'I believe the Prosecution's questions were designed to determine whether or not your client is subject to hallucinations. Am I correct?'

'Yes, your Honour.'

'Please continue your interrogation.'

At first glance, it's very simple. The Flat is on the sixth floor . . . But once you're outside, how can you possibly close the window behind you? Leave a note to apologise for creating a draught? No . . . No notes. Not a trace. Don't put them to the trouble of picking up and trying to fit together the disarticulated members of your body and your speech. Legs where arms should be, objects for subjects, heads for genitives, adjectals for verbs . . .

100

There's no way to make this add up to anything, it's perfectly incoherent, the key is missing.

In actual fact, it's very difficult. If only someone else. If only – abdicate even that decision. If only the patter of steps behind Omaya, in the street, would get louder and louder, faster and faster, and turn out to be the patter of a machine gun.

The gavel slices through the air and strikes. The voices are extinguished. Darkness and expectant silence reign. Omaya is waiting, motionless, at the centre of the stage. The curtain goes up. The circle of light descends upon her. Blinded, she starts talking.

In detective films, they always shine a bright light directly into the face of the criminal. Blinded, he starts talking. The projectors give off a hot light that causes make-up to melt, masks to fall away, falsehoods to collapse. The light ferrets out the truth, hounding it into a corner. You cannot see your judges, those to whom you have to tell the truth, but they can see you. Your stark nakedness, your stark terror. The headlights shining on the rabbit . . . No, there weren't any headlights.

Omaya has stopped speaking. The circle of light has grown indistinct, gradually mingling with the footlights. Saroyan has come to join me. We've rehearsed this scene a hundred times at his place, amidst cushions and wall-hangings and cups of tea. I'm playing the Vamp, my body is hard and black and brilliant. I turn away from Saroyan and move upstage towards a spiral staircase, he tries to restrain me, runs after me and grabs me by the shoulders, between that moment and Saroyan's scream I don't remember a thing, he screams whereas there's no mention of a scream at that point in the script, the audience musn't suspect that anything is wrong, Omaya starts to ascend the spiral staircase, one hand lifting her black dress slit to the thigh, and only when the rising curve of steps brings her back round to face the audience does she see Saroyan's body, Saroyan's curled-up, whimpering body, and understand that even this last respite has been snatched from her, that even on stage she will never again be in control ... Saroyan manages to patch up some kind of plausibility, the ovation that night is like machine-gun patter, Omaya shuts her eyes, relieved to find herself in front of the firing squad at last, but when the clapping has died down she's still alive, she has to face up to Saroyan, the other actors, the director, and gradually she comes to realise, to reconstruct: *it was her stiletto heel.*

I musn't play that role any more. I'm too nervous, it's the role that makes me nervous, I'm terribly sorry, I didn't do it on purpose, I swear, it wasn't at all premeditated, I didn't mean any harm, either to Saroyan or to the show, replace me, forgive me, but don't exclude me, oh please, please don't throw me out.

'What do you mean, you didn't do it on purpose?'

'I swear, it wasn't at all premeditated.'

'Not on purpose and not premeditated are two different things. One doesn't just carry off a silver necklace by accident.'

'I meant to pay for it, I swear I did, and then I must have got distracted for a moment . . .'

'And you walked distractedly out of the store after having distractedly stuffed the necklace into the bottom of your bag?'

'I'd opened the bag to look for a tissue . . .'

'And while you were wiping your nose, the necklace

slithered insidiously like a snake beneath your diary, your wallet, your tissues and the rest?'

He didn't say that. He certainly can't have said insidiously like a snake.

'Thus, your client lost her innocence long ago. Her police record, years before the fateful month of December, was far from pristine. Clerk, be sure you've got this down correctly: the young lady had displayed anti-social behaviour on previous occasions. Moreover, she had concocted flagrant lies to avoid being brought to court.'

'The petty thefts committed by my client cannot be said to bespeak a criminal attitude; rather, they were the sign of a slight psychological disturbance. At one time in her life, she did have a tendency towards kleptomania, but this tendency subsided after treatment and eventually disappeared. Allow me to remind you, moreover, that in the present case my client was not the perpetrator of an assault but the victim of one, and that the circumstances of the crime have not yet been fully brought to light.'

'Objection, your Honour . . . It's far from being established that a crime was committed. My colleague behaves as though your judgement had already been given. Her intention in so doing is to influence the opinion of the jury. I demand that she withdraw her assertion immediately.'

'Objection sustained.'

'Call the accused.'
No one said that. But what? What did they say? Call . . . There's a word for it . . .
'Call the prisoner.'

No, that's not it, either. You're not being held prisoner here, young lady. No one is detaining you. Your situation might be called confinement, but it hasn't yet become incarceration. If you don't like it here, instead of complaining all the time . . .

That's it:

'Call the plaintiff.'

The one who's constantly complaining, about anything and everything. Lack of sleep, lack of appetite, lack of love, lack of humour, lack of integrity, lack of orientation, lack of keys.

'Stop whining, you'll drive me crazy. Oh come on, darling, don't start blubbering now. Show me your hand. How did you hurt yourself?'

'The knife did it, it cut Omaya's finger, it gave her a wound.'

'Where? *Where*? I can't see anything at all.'

'Right there! You see? It's right there! Owwwwww, it hurts, it hurts . . .'

'*That*? You call that a wound? That tiny little red spot? But it isn't even bleeding! Listen, darling, you're not a baby any more, you mustn't cry about such little things. Run a bit of cold water over it, if you like. But be a darling and leave me alone for a while, I have some work to finish before I go to bed. You can get off to sleep all by yourself, can't you, my big girl?'

'Mightn't that be the source of your problem with cutting instruments? Eternally reliving that scene in the hopes that it might turn out differently – by the acknowledgment of your pain?'

Omaya is lying on the couch. She is knitting. Behind her,

above her, Saroyan. He is her husband. He is talking to her, using words written by someone else. He is telling her he loves another woman. Omaya feels feigned jealousy rising within her, feigned anger bringing her blood to the boil. She gets to her feet, spins around and plunges the knitting-needle into her husband's chest. Saroyan collapses. He is dead. The knitting-needle is real.

'That's a lie. That's nothing but a pack of lies. I would never have done a thing like that. How could I have murdered Saroyan? He was my friend. The only man I've ever trusted.'

'There was that previous incident with the stiletto heel . . .'

'That was an accident! It was due to a moment's distraction! But this time you're trying to charge me with a crime I know nothing about!'

'So how do you explain the fact that your friend is dead?'

'He's not dead, he's just pretending. He's acting. It's in the script. His character is supposed to die. He's waiting for the applause, and since no one is clapping he doesn't want to get up. Isn't that right, Saroyan?'

Saroyan doesn't move.

'So even when a man doesn't move, he can knock you up. What a fascinating discovery.'

'Don't be sarcastic, Alix. That really isn't what I need right now. I need your help.'

'Men for love, and women for assistance. How charming. You got yourself into this bloody mess, you can get yourself out of it. I don't see why I should help you wash your dirty linen in public.'

'Give us the precise meaning of the following expression: to wash one's dirty linen in public.'

'No! Not now . . . I'm with Alix. Alix is protecting me. She's driving me to the clinic.'

'What does the proud father have to say about it? Is he enthusiastic about your nipping his child in the bud?'

'No, he isn't . . . He says it would do me good to have a child.'

'Immortal wisdom.'

'He says it would calm me down, make me think about somebody else, be less obsessed with myself . . . If I had to deal with some indisputable reality, then maybe my . . . my . . . the rest of it would torment me a bit less.'

'How benevolent of him. Is that why he didn't want to drive you to the clinic? So as not to be an accomplice to the crime you're about to commit?'

'You know very well Saroyan doesn't have a car. Stop it, Alix, please . . . It's hard enough already.'

Put your feet in the stirrups. Spread your legs as far apart as you can.

This, I'll never get over. This is irreparable.

Omaya and Saroyan are married. They have a little girl two and a half years old. On a regular basis, the government gives all parents the option of putting their offspring to death. Omaya is discussing with Saroyan the decision they should take concerning their daughter. She tries to sound him out and anticipate his wishes. She hesitates, ventures a Yes? and Saroyan nods his head: All right. It shall be done.

The parents are legally obliged to attend the ceremony. It entails placing the sleeping child on a slab of stone, laying a smaller stone upon its body to hold it down, and then lowering the whole thing, by means of a pulley, into a vault especially designed for the purpose. The grave-digger is an old man with wizened skin and knotty hands. He carries out the necessary steps, totally impassive. At the end, when the slab of stone has reached the bottom, he sprinkles a handful of sulphate on the baby's body so it will consume itself once buried.

As soon as it is over, Omaya is flooded with remorse. She thinks back to her pregnancy, the thrilled impatience with which she and Saroyan had waited for the child, she remembers the delivery, all that suffering for nothing, and it dawns on her that two and a half years don't add up to a lifetime, they don't add up to anything at all – it is monstrous. On her knees, Omaya implores Saroyan to reverse their decision. She says they've made a terrible mistake, they must do everything in their power to correct it, and Saroyan nods his head: All right.

Together they run to find the grave-digger and he agrees, somewhat begrudgingly, to make the rescue attempt. He seeks out a doctor to accompany him to the bottom of the vault. When the two men return to the surface, they inform us that the baby hasn't died yet, it might survive, only . . .

'Only what?'

'Only . . . the sulphate has already started to burn its chest . . . it's left a wound . . .'

'Yes? Go on.'

'They ask me to guess the shape of the wound. They tell me: It's in the shape of a letter, guess which one?'

'What happened next? Don't cry, it's just a dream. What shape was the wound?'

'It was in the shape . . . of an O.'

'But that's only natural, it doesn't mean anything. All

wounds are shaped like Os. Everything tends towards roundness, you know that. The bubbles beneath the ice, your father's trajectory around the lake, the mouths of the child prisoners when they sing . . . It's only to be expected!'

It's just a dream, a fairy-tale, a sentimental novel. What happened, essentially, is nothing at all. Omaya didn't really murder Saroyan, she's never been pregnant. she doesn't even know how to knit. The whole thing is just a story, a play, a phantasmagoria. What happened, essentially, is nothing at all. Omaya doesn't know how to create things, her only art is words in the air, and apart from that she's sterile. Fundamentally incapable of fashioning anything real.

A sculptress, the sister of a famous writer, the mistress of a still more famous sculptor, hacks furiously away at marble blocks; from them she extorts kisses and secrets, waltzes and blood-curdling screams. She falls ill and they tell her she mustn't sculpt any more. They lock her up in a Castle and she writes to her brother: Get me out of here, help me to get out, the years are passing and I'm growing old, she grows old and gives up hope, she never leaves the Castle, it's not her brother but her death that finally delivers her.

Stop it. Stop – the – train – has stopped. Three boys get on. The horde has long since vanished. These are older boys, they might almost be mistaken for men, they have everything they need in order to be men, the right height, the whiskers, the bass voice, but you can tell they're not men because all these features are slightly exaggerated: the bodies stretch a bit too far upwards, the voices drop a bit too far downwards, the cheeks are ostentatiously hirsute, therefore these must be boys who are playing at being men, men are nothing but grown-up children, one of them is not quite as tall as the other two, there are three of them, there were three of them, can you describe them to us, one of them was shorter than the other two, he's the scapegoat, this schoolboy is the scapegoat of his class-mates, particularly of the taller one who jostles him constantly, before the doors have closed he's pushed him out of the train onto the platform five times but the short boy laughs, he mustn't get angry or he'll risk losing the taller boys' esteem, he has to prove that he can take it, without seeming to take it just because he's shorter than they are and therefore has no choice, so he just laughs, he says cut it out, cut it out I said, will you bloody well cut it out, the fifth time his laugh starts sounding forced, you can see the panic breaking in his eyes, how will he ever manage to save face if they keep at him like this with everyone watching, but fortunately just then the doors slide shut, and the tallest boy will have to invent a new game, a new form of torture for the shortest one . . .

Cut it out. The words are there in black and white, right next to Omaya. I can see them. They're really there. They're printed at the top of a right-hand page, next to the well-groomed fingernail of a man. At the top of the left-hand page is the name of the book's author, a name synonymous with best-seller. Cut it out, says the black woman. Omaya don't read that, please stop. I told you to suck me off, says the black man. The words file down the page, one after the other. They are words. The black man picks up a sabre and cuts off the black woman's head. Stop. The black man holds the black woman's bleeding head by the hair, and even before the bottom of the page he has got what he wanted. Five hundred thousand copies. Five hundred thousand printings of: Cut it out, says the black woman. Five hundred thousand readings of: I told you to suck me off, says the black man. The white thumb turns the page. Omaya turns her head.

'Can I drive you somewhere?'
'No, thank you.'
'Come on, don't be scared. You look tired, I feel like doing you a favour. Full stop – that's all there is to it.'
'I'd prefer to walk. Thanks anyway.'
'It's because I'm black, isn't it? You're a bloody racist, aren't you?'
'I just feel like walking by myself.'

Omaya shuts her eyes. These are words. Everything I've been telling you is words.

With my eyes shut, I never know if I'm sitting facing the front or the back of the train. If it's the front, we must be going north, if it's the back, we must be going south. The north is always directly ahead of you when you look at a map. The south behind you and the east to the right and the west to the left. A living compass. They turned right, then right again, then left. East, east, west. Why didn't you try to find out where you were? When did you notice they weren't in fact driving you back to the Castle?

'You're starting to hesitate before you answer. Quick – what is the exact meaning of the following expression: he who hesitates is lost?'
'He who hesitates is lost, that means that those who never hesitate never get lost, there's no way they can be led off the track, they'll go all the way, they'll get what they

want, you can try any number of ploys to throw them off the scent, nothing will do any good, they'll just keep plunging straight ahead, ever northwards, whatever obstacles may be set in their paths.'

'That's fine. In fact, that's rather good. So I gather that you yourself have suffered from a lack of orientation in what might be called your . . . er . . . professional life?'

'I'm sorry . . . I didn't quite grasp the meaning of your question.'

'Would you consider yourself a fallen woman?'

It was the Owl who taught me how to orient myself by the stars. He could see in the dark. He didn't even need headlights, his night vision was so perfect. Thanks to the stars, you can never get lost, as long as it's night-time and as long as the sky isn't cloudy and as long as going northwards means going where you want to go. He was walking in the forest and I was following him. It was only natural that he should be the guide, with his head so full of constellations his eyes were twinkling, and that I should draw up behind, my eyes on the ground so as not to step on thorns, trip up on roots and plunge forward onto sharp stones. I was following him and I was happy because he was singing, the song of the owl is filled with wisdom, I was listening and his wisdom was floating gently into my ears, I had to be careful not to listen too closely or else I would forget to look where I was going, I'd fall and then the Owl would go on without me and I'd be left behind, a fallen woman. But suddenly he stopped. I bumped into him in the dark. He took me by the hand. I could see that his eyes were studying the sky. The stars had stopped twinkling and his eyes had become vacant. We were in the middle of the forest in the middle of the night and the sky was full of clouds and so was his head and so was mine.

'Haven't we already passed this oak tree before? Do you recognise it?'

Why does he ask me if I recognise it, I don't want to answer, I don't know the right answer, he's the guide, I have nothing to do with cognition or recognition . . .

'Listen . . . Can you hear the cars on the road? We have to try and get our bearings, the stars have disappeared.'

Why does he ask me to listen, I don't want to hear anything but his song, I don't want to learn anything that's not already part of his wisdom. Why does he ask me to help him, it's his job to help me, an Owl can't be lost, that's a contradiction in terms . . .

If you go in circles round a lake, it's impossible to get lost. From now on I'll always know where the Owl is, and so will he, but the stars have gone out. And I keep moving forwards to the north and backwards to the south, always along the same line but all the landmarks have disappeared, I've lost my straight ahead. I progress and I regress and it doesn't change a thing.

'What was your client's address before she entered the Castle?'

'She'd had no fixed address for several weeks prior to her admission. The theatre company with which she'd been working had disbanded, she was unemployed and could no longer pay her rent. Therefore she was put up by various friends.'

'Why, then, did you recount the scene with Saroyan in which he offered to cue the plaintiff for the new play?'

'That scene was vital for understanding Saroyan's character.'

'You mean you made it up from beginning to end?'

'Of course not. It was a combination of several

encounters that actually took place between my client and her friend.'

'Very well. Clerk, please take note: the plaintiff's lawyer admits to having considerably altered the facts during the first hearing. Now, to continue: these ... er ... friends who put the plaintiff up during the weeks prior to her incarceration – were they men? Or women?'

'Both. Mostly women.'

'Would you say that during this period your client manifested symptoms of being a fallen woman?'

'Not at all.'

'And yet you just stated that she was circulating among various friends, sleeping with one and then another?'

'I see no connection between these questions and the task at hand, namely to establish as rigorously as possible not the past history of my client but the exact circumstances of the assault perpetrated against her.'

'Would it be possible to call one of these so-called friends to the witness stand?'

Saroyan won't come. He'll never move again. I saw it with my own eyes: they placed him on a slab of stone, laid a smaller stone up on his body to hold it down, and then lowered the whole thing by means of a pulley into a vault especially designed for the purpose. Finally, they scattered a handful of sulphate on Saroyan's body so it would consume itself once buried. There are some substances which speed up the ageing process and others which slow it down. Sulphate makes it go pretty fast, but don't worry, the onslaught of age can be withstood thanks to anti-wrinkle cream. Never forget: at night, more than at any other time, you need to be beautiful. Never remove your make-up at this crucial moment. And if you hope to captivate, never go to bed without applying a fresh layer of anti-wrinkle cream. It's colourless and odourless: your husband won't suspect a thing. He'll see nothing but your face – your true face, the one that enchanted him the day you first met.

Before love, keep your eyes open, avoid smiling, raising your eyebrows or frowning, don't speak too loudly, drink lots of water, don't smoke, get regular exercise, eat fresh fruits and vegetables, watch your waistline, be cheerful but don't smile too much. During love, close your eyes, don't frown, don't scream too loudly, hold your stomach in, tighten your buttocks, harden your breasts, avoid smiling. Of course, passionate kisses may smear your make-up a bit: don't let that bother you. Mascara and eye-liner are intended to evoke black eyes. Eye-shadow, especially in shades of blue and mauve, is highly suggestive of bruises. The purpose of lipstick is to create the illusion that your mouth is bleeding. If it gets a little smeared around the lips, the effect will only be heightened. Same for the other lips. A bit of rouge, a bit of blood can only enhance your charms. Indeed, it is common knowledge that nothing arouses male ardour more effectively than women in the middle of their period.

'Excuse me, I'm conducting a survey on women in your situation. Could you tell me whether or not you had your period at the time?'

'Thus, you claim to have seen a scarlet droplet on your thigh. What were the dates of your last period – and are you regular, as a general rule?'

'I'm sorry . . . I'm not sure I quite understood the question.'

'Do you know the rules and regulations, yes or no? Let me see your ticket.'

'My ticket?'

'You can't go anywhere without a regulation ticket. I must have some sort of written evidence.'

'Evidence?'

'We're accustomed to judging each case on the evidence. You're not allowed to travel without papers.'

'You mean . . . identification papers? You want me to furnish proof of my identity?'

'Identity or difference, it hardly matters, provided that your photograph is attached and your signature appended.'

'Wait a minute. I have some cards in my wallet, let me show you what I have.'

'You're wasting my time, I'm going to have to charge you.'

'Charge me . . .?'

'What is your name? . . . Your address? . . . Can you at least tell me which neighbourhood you live in? Would you be capable of pointing it out to me on a map of the city? Would you even be capable of drawing me a map of the city? How long have you been living here? Hurry up, hurry up, I have no time to waste. How many times per week do you take this train? We're conducting a survey of railway passengers. If one train leaves the station at four in the afternoon and travels at an average speed of ninety miles an hour, and another train leaves the same station at seven in the evening and travels at an average speed of one hundred and twenty miles an hour, how long will it take for the second train to catch up with the first? Hurry up, hurry up: every second's hesitation will cost you one point.'

Cybele wouldn't hesitate. Answers are always there for her, at her fingertips, at her beck and call, docile and obedient. How many calories should a fourteen-year-old girl consume each day? How much pocket money should she be given each week? Numbers answer Cybele politely whenever she asks them a question, and their answers are irrefutable. Every problem has its solution, provided that you formulate it correctly, taking all the variables into account . . .

'Excuse me, Miss. Does this train stop anywhere near City Hall?'

The answer exists, it's either yes or no, near means less than a ten-minute walk, near means this body, sitting down next to mine on purpose whereas there are empty seats all around; near means this mouth, lying when it claims not to know the train's route, lying when it smiles in asking me the question.

'Don't you feel like talking? What's the matter? Got problems?'

 . . .

'The least you could do is give us a smile.'

He himself has stopped smiling. Omaya stares at a tiny rip in the empty seat across from her. Disappear into the crack. Never come out of the wound alive . . . Frozen. And this time Alix not here. The paralysis worse, even worse. The back as rigid as a dead branch, the bones about to snap . . .

'Smile, you bitch.'

If only he'd go away, if only he'd content himself with bitch, with just the voice, not the hand, not the hand . . .

'You're too ugly anyway.'

He's stalked off in disgust. And Omaya's body is throbbing, the blood is hurling itself against the skin from the inside, trying to spurt out through the pores, and Omaya is buffeted and thrashed about from head to foot,

116

her muscles melt, her joints go soft, her face becomes obscenely permeable, open to any wind, to any bacteria, any infection . . .

'Today we begin our work on the Plague. I've prepared a list of documents on the subject for you to read. This reading is compulsory, but the script of the play will not derive from it directly. In the course of the coming days and months, you will have to find the words you need yourselves in order to act – that is, in this case, in order to survive. Each of you will create a character using the concrete information provided by the documents. For the first couple of weeks, you'll live within the character's healthy body. Following this, you'll start to feel – through *that body* rather than your own – the developing symptoms of the illness.

The first buboes form in the neck, the underarms and the loins. They start out as a slight irritation, then a tiny lump appears, then two, and finally several red, purulent lumps. Your skin is raw. You lift your arms so as not to exacerbate the pain. You walk with your legs apart. Clothes become a veritable torture . . . and yet, you mustn't let it show. You're suffering atrociously, but no one must be allowed to see. The sick can be distinguished from the well at a distance, by the way they walk. Suspicion and hatred spread even more quickly than the disease itself. The sick suspect their loved ones of having contaminated them, the well flee their loved ones as a potential source of death. Pity, tenderness, fraternity are eaten away, egoism holds absolute sway. Parents abandon their infants, condemned lovers tear at each other's throats, panic gradually takes hold of the entire village . . . but it's an *individual* panic, impossible to share: every human being you meet is a mortal enemy.'

117

Omaya works alone. There is no script, no landmark. She doesn't go walking in the forest, she doesn't settle in at Saroyan's, she remains shut up at home. For ten days. Naked. She reads. And as she reads, she eats. She only gets dressed and leaves the Flat in order to buy bread. She devours page after page and loaf after loaf. The curtains are drawn, she leaves the electric light on, she sleeps sitting up in the armchair with a book and a loaf in her lap, she wakes without knowing whether it is day or night, she reads, she eats. She feels the gradual swelling of her flesh. She sees her stomach, thighs and arms puff up. She's turning into a baker. Her white skin is a permanent layer of flour over her body. After ten days, she finally gets dressed. She returns to the Theatre and recognises no one.

The baker has already seen her children succumb: thirst, fever, swollen glands, vomiting, death, she knows the whole process by heart. She knows that she herself is now ripe for suffering. Her body is a huge white loaf about to go mouldy. Green and mauve mildew will settle onto Omaya and start carrying out its task of destruction.

The other people need me, they need my bread in order not to die, and I – I need their money. I show them only the whitest, plumpest parts: my back, my calves, a breast, a buttock. Come, take, eat! They don't suspect that what I give them to consume is infected, baked in the oven of fever, that the fragments of white food I hand them are already spoiled. I smile, despite the intolerable burning of the hidden spots of green and mauve.

They're convinced the whole thing must be their fault. They wonder what sin they can possibly have committed to deserve to see their children die like flies. Children can't resist my sugared wares. My own vanished one after the other, six in all, the baby was the first to go, then my eldest son, then the twins, all of them, every one, piled onto the wagon, I'd hear the bell go clang, and why should the other children continue to play in the streets when my own are decomposing in the common grave? So I entice them on purpose and I poison them, I can hear their parents lamenting – *mea culpa, mea culpa, mea maxima culpa* – and I laugh and I rejoice, pray all you want, repent all you want, your gods have nothing to do with this, I'm the all-powerful from now on, I'm the one who deals out death left and right, and I'll win out in the end because I am your food and satisfaction, I am your rot and putrefaction, and only rot can possibly survive, I'll be the last of us alive.

Saroyan is black and scrawny next to fat, white Omaya. The character he's concocted is some kind of solicitor or scrivener, dressed in a tattered tailcoat and a lopsided top-hat, he's like a weird crow when he swoops down on the baker's fine white bread, pecking nastily at my throat to get the very softest crumbs. And the others, all those beggars who'd like to eat me for nothing, and their bellows of despair when I refuse. And the village doctor, ailing himself – he's the one who finally caught on; with his last drop of strength he seized a giant bread-knife and split me from head to foot – that was Roman.

'We can't prevent them. They have the right to call whatever witnesses they want.'

'And Roman has agreed to testify?'

'Yes . . . But there's no reason why his testimony should do you any harm. It's just as likely to absolve you.'

'Absolve me?'

'How long have you known the plaintiff?'

'About a year and a half. I joined the company very shortly before it broke up. So we only worked together

119

once, during the show on the Plague.'

'Following the company's disbanding, the plaintiff stayed in your flat for two weeks – is that correct?'

'You have excellent informers.'

'Answer the question.'

'That is correct.'

'During this period, did you live as man and wife?'

'Not at all.'

'You do grasp the meaning of my question, don't you? Did you have marital relations with the plaintiff, either before or during or after the time you lived with her?'

'The answer is no. The plaintiff always slept sitting up in an armchair.'

'In your opinion, was the plaintiff a fallen woman?'

'I have no idea what that expression means.'

'To your knowledge, was the plaintiff a person of dubious morals? Did her . . . er . . . intimate behaviour . . . er . . . deviate from the norm?'

. . .

'Allow me to remind you that you are under oath.'

'I remember one day, your Honour . . .'

'Yes?'

'One day last summer . . . We'd just given a matinee performance. The audience had been quite enthralled, the actors were euphoric . . . The plaintiff and I left the Theatre together. It was pouring with rain, a wonderful warm summer shower. The plaintiff still had flour in her hair – in the play she was a baker – and she took a bottle of shampoo from her toilet bag . . .'

'Yes?'

'Well, with all due respect, she asked me to wash her hair in the rain. She lay down on the concrete in the car park . . . It was raining so hard our clothes were sticking to our skin, we were laughing uproariously . . . I soaped her

120

head and rubbed her scalp, the rain took care of the rinsing, the lather went running down her face and neck . . . The plaintiff was ecstatic.'

'Yes, and then?'

'That's all, your Honour, honestly. That is the sum total of my knowledge concerning this individual's deviant intimate behaviour.'

Marvellous Roman . . . Alix wasn't called as a witness last time, but maybe today . . . Oh Alix, it was you I would have liked to call that evening, but between you and me so many obstacles, so many men and cars and telephones and streets . . . If only I could have heard the sound of your voice, I would have known . . . what? You didn't love me any more, you hadn't come to see me at the Castle, you were angry with me for being so defeated, for having misplaced all my keys and landmarks, in your eyes that was unforgivable.

'Did the plaintiff stay at your apartment during the autumn preceding her incarceration?'

'No, Ma'am. We'd broken up during the insufferable spring.'

'And had you been in contact with the plaintiff since your break-up?'

'Yes, Ma'am. Omaya would call me on the phone from time to time, but we had nothing left to say to each other. I advise you to sentence her to a good fifteen years in prison. She loves being locked up. For her, an honest-to-goodness prison would be heaven on earth. At last she'd be able to give herself over completely to her favourite activity, which is passivity.'

Alix didn't say that, she'd never say a thing like that, she's incapable of the slightest cruelty.

'So why do you keep making up this kind of scene?'

'She was given a life with immediate entry . . .'

'Whereas you were given . . .'

. . .

'A life with no instruction booklet? No keys? No advance training courses? Wouldn't it be more accurate to say that you did possess the keys at one time, but had them spirited away from you? Don't you want to lodge a complaint for theft?'

'I challenge the validity of these allegations. Nothing was stolen. This woman didn't belong to anyone. There was no sign saying PRIVATE PROPERTY. And how can one steal public property? That is nonsense. There's no case for it.'

'Please summon the witness for the defence.'

'. . . How long have you known the accused?'

'Nearly fifteen years.'

'What is the nature of your relationship?'

'At first it was a professional relationship, so to speak, and then a friendly one, if I may say so – in all modesty, of course.'

'Please give us your version of the facts.'

'Well, I met the accused at his garage, I'd brought my car in because it needed a few repairs, I went back the next day to see how the work was getting on, little by little we started chatting and we found each other, well . . . quite amenable. I can say in all sincerity that the accused is a reliable man who takes his job seriously and does it well. I'm pretty interested in cars myself, so we've had lots of good talks . . .'

'When you state that the accused is a reliable man, do

you mean that he would be unlikely, for example, to ask to have his hair washed in the rain in the city centre?'

'Oh, yes, Ma'am, I can guarantee that. He'd never do such a thing. Or the other thing, for that matter. Maybe a drink or two from time to time, I won't deny that. He enjoyed fraternising. But he's basically a very responsible person. That's the main thing I'd have to say about him: he's a very responsible person.'

'Thank you, Sir. Your Honour, I'd like your permission to interrogate the plaintiff once again.'

'Permission granted.'

'Young lady . . . Could you tell the court when you last washed your hair?'

'I . . . what? When I what?'

'What is the date of your most recent shampoo? Take your time. Think it over carefully before you answer.'

'I don't need to think it over. I washed my hair this morning.'

'And how do you account for that fact?'

'I . . . well, I . . . I've washed my hair every morning since . . . since quite a while ago . . . it never seems to be clean enough . . . At the Castle, I'd often lock myself in the shower while breakfast was being served and wash my hair . . .'

'Thank you very much. In your opinion, Ladies and Gentlemen of the jury, does this behaviour not betray the plaintiff's obvious and excessive coquetry? She admits to having washed her hair *every single day* – since long *before* the events took place. I ask you: what reason could a woman possibly have to pay such excessive attention to her appearance, if not to turn men's heads and whet the flames of their desire?'

If you insert the pins horizontally, parallel to the scalp,

taking great care to attach only one lock of hair with each pin, and if you then wait until your hair is completely dry, you'll have lovely curls that will stay in place all day long, provided that there's no wind and that you don't wear a scarf on your head and that no one comes along and tousles your hair affectionately. If, on the other hand, you insert the pins vertically, perpendicular to the scalp, they'll pass through the skull and stimulate various regions of the brain. It is a well-known fact that pleasure and pain are rather vague notions and that one is easily mistaken for the other. In the course of scientific experiments conducted in our laboratory, we were able to artificially provoke these supposedly contrary sensations by stimulating sections of the brain that were a mere few-hundredths of an inch apart. If the plaintiff claims to have experienced pain, therefore, it is quite possible that this impression was the result of a *minimal* displacement with respect to her actual experience, namely pleasure. Moreover, since it is a well-known fact that women, when they feel pain, often simulate pleasure, the opposite must be equally true: that when they feel pleasure, they can simulate pain. In the present case, I would say, this hypothesis is extremely likely.

No one said that.

In the Castle, certain keyless men had long white scars at the bases of their skulls. Idiotic grins that went from one ear to the other. They were calm. You'd never see them around the wings near the exit, always much further inside, at the very back of the garden, where the high walls covered with barbed-wire met at right angles. It was said that one of these men – but this was long before my time – had died of tetanus. Strong and slender, he'd managed to shin up to the top of the wall with his arms full of roses, and he'd spent the night attaching the flowers to the prickly, rusted, poisonous stems; the iron thorns had lacerated his forearms so badly that he couldn't be saved. That was one of the legends of the Castle. Another had it that a keyless man – this time a scarless one – had succeeded in impregnating a woman who'd never had a key in her life. She herself was unaware of what had happened: it was the nurse who noticed her untouched pile of sanitary napkins and arranged for the stifling of the scandal, that is to say of the potential child, with the potential mother meanwhile under an anaesthetic scarcely more general than that of her usual state . . .

And now, as if on cue, a fat dairy cow sits down opposite me. In the underground one must give up one's seat to pregnant women. She aims her uterus at Omaya like a rifle. So sure of her right to sit there, to take up all the space, to splay her legs apart, she spreads out, superb and hideous, triumphant. Narrow blue viperine snakes are crawling up her calves, teeming like living vermicelli . . . No! They can't . . . No, Omaya, they're motionless, look at her face instead . . . But on her face, countless brown stains and blotches, patches of plague sticking to her cheeks and getting bigger by the second, before long her whole face will be covered with purulent scabs, it starts in the neck, the underarms and the loins, and then it spreads inexorably through the body, it starts in the loins, the infection takes root there, and then it spreads throughout the body, there's nothing you can do about it, a man takes you, he injects his poison into your loins, and then you feel the buboes as the glands begin to swell, that's why the baker jubilantly dealt out death, she wanted her revenge, she wanted the others to feel what she had felt, six times in

125

a row, the slow invasion of the illness, the viperine snakes teeming in her legs, the constant irrepressible itching, it starts in the loins and it ends by killing you.

The dairy cow draws a book from her bag, opens it at the page with the folded corner, props it up on her uterus and begins to read. On the cover a tall dark-haired man has his arms around a small light-haired woman, he's in profile and you can see the hard line of his chin, she's full face and you can see the soft line of her smile, I know what words the fat cow is absorbing this very moment, the folded corner was near the beginning of the book so the light-haired woman is saying: Please stop, and the man is saying: You little idiot, you know you enjoyed it, and the woman is saying Stop, but the man is sealing her lips with his, bruising them with his teeth, rummaging in her mouth with his tongue, and the cow's lips start to form the same insipid smile as the heroine's, and this will go on for a hundred pages more, at which point a diamond will at last make clear to us why, though she keeps repeating Stop, the heroine is smiling, it's because diamonds are the hardest things in the world. The dairy cow is not wearing a diamond, not even the least circle of gold, most likely her fingers have swollen and she doesn't want to cut off her circulation, yet that's exactly what circles of gold are for, to cut off circulation, and if they aren't worn around the ring-finger they can be hooked into the woman's very body, for example by boring a hole through her earlobe or through her nose or through her clitoris; then again it's possible to solder not just one but several dozen golden rings around her neck, one for each year, so that when the woman is of marriageable age she'll have a magnificent giraffe's neck, twice its normal length, and all these circles mean that the circulation has been cut off, that the woman has been withdrawn from circulation, and if she persists in

126

circulating after her wedding all the rings will be removed at once, and her neck, having neither muscles nor vertebrae to support the weight of the head, will break.

'What is it about circles that you find so terrifying? The bubbles beneath the ice, your father's trajectory around the lake, the prisoners' mouths open in song, your own initial burned into the skin of your child, and now this dreadful imagery of rings?'

'It's not my job to interpret.'

'Naturally not. You must be curious to know my opinion. Curiosity killed the cat – what is the meaning of that saying? Come on, hurry up and answer!'

'Curiosity killed the cat, that means that when a cat wants to have babies, she finds herself some dark hiding-place, down in the basement, for example, yes, in a cardboard box high up on a shelf in the basement, and you search for her everywhere, you call her name frantically, at last you hear her mewing in reply, you think she must be playing hide-and-seek, you grab the box and turn it upside-down, you shake it as hard as you can, the cat falls to the ground and smashes into bits. Omaya screams. Then the fragments of cat start crawling around on the cold cement floor, they squirm and bob their heads, they're little kittens and the mother is seeking desperately to reassemble them, to bring them back beneath her warm body, and in the end she finds them all . . . All but one.'

'Why all but one?'

'Because the last little one is dead. Curiosity has killed her. Omaya screams and screams. I killed her, I killed her.'

'No, you didn't, darling, it's not your fault.'

'Yes, it is, I threw them all on the ground, I didn't know,

I didn't even know she was expecting, I though she must be hiding on me and I turned the box upside-down!'

'But look, darling, look at the little kitten, you didn't kill her. She's all sticky, you see? She's still covered with fluid.'

'What does that mean?'

'It means she was stillborn, since her mummy didn't even bother to lick her clean. You didn't kill her, the others are doing fine, you see? You didn't hurt them in the least.'

So a mother can bring a child into the world and then not even bother to lick her clean. So a mother can bring a child into the world and be indifferent to her: without even trying to revive her, she can leave her lying there, a tiny black heap, moist and motionless on the icy basement floor . . .

'But when I take the plane I don't leave you behind, Omaya, I'm always by your side, you're always by my side, that's what's so wonderful about the human brain, you can take your loved ones with you in your thoughts, even if you can't take them with you in flesh and blood.'

'I'd rather be left behind than taken along in someone's thoughts in an aeroplane and then digested by a computer.'

'That's absurd.'

'That's outrageous. Besides, how did you know the stillborn kitten was female? Are you sure of it? What makes you so convinced? The same thing goes for the episode at dusk: how could you possibly have known it was a female rabbit? Well? Have you any proof? And what about your own femaleness – have you proof of that? Have you fulfilled your duty as a mother?'

'That's absurd, Omaya. You'll understand better when you have children of your own.'
'Then I'll never understand.'

Cybele's plane has landed, the airport is in a suburb not far from the one in which the court is located, she'll hop into a limousine and get there before I do, she'll be waiting for me in the hall, just as anxiously as the last time, she'll put her arms around me and hug me tight, so tight my neck will nearly break.

'Oh, Omaya. Oh my baby. Don't you want to drop your complaint? After all the time that's gone by . . . Do you want to go on living in hell? Look at the rings beneath your eyes, it hurts me to see you in such a state. My darling, I know you were badly wounded by what happened, but you're the one who persists in reopening the wound. Otherwise it might have healed over by now . . . don't you think? Listen, wouldn't it be better for you just to forget the whole thing?'

'Not until it's been acknowledged there's a whole thing to forget. Don't you see? How does one go about forgetting nothing? How does one go about healing a wound in the shape of an O? I must talk to Anastasia. Let me go. Let go of me, Cybele.'

'Are you ready?'
'I'm not feeling well.'
'I can see that. You must try and get hold of yourself. Everything will go just fine. Try not to live through it in advance. Is your mother here?'
'Yes . . . why?'
'They might want to question her.'

'My *mother*?'

'Yes. Just a question of aetiology.'

'What?'

'Just a question of deontology. Moral antecedents and the like.'

'You're the parent of the plaintiff, you're the one who brought her into the world?'

'Into the world, yes, in the midst of pain, Omaya bursting forth from the wound.'

'Please restrict yourself to answering the questions you are asked, without literary embellishments. Could you please describe to the court, in succinct terms, the genesis of her illness?'

'It goes back a long time, to when Omaya was just a little girl and started having attacks of asthma. The attacks would usually occur when she was in the vicinity of cats, whereas, up until then, cats had been her favourite animals.'

'Even at the time, then, her disorder was of a psycho-somatic, not to say somapsychotic, nature?'

'If you like.'

'How long did these attacks persist?'

'They never actually stopped. Up until puberty, they tended to be relatively mild; all we had to do was remove the cats and Omaya would be able to breathe again. During her adolescence, the attacks grew more and more violent and unpredictable; they no longer seemed to have any direct relation either to cats or to any other visible source of bronchial irritation. We were therefore obliged to start medicinal treatment of her respiratory tracts.'

'And did this undertaking meet with success?'

'Yes and no. The medicine, while quite effective in stopping the illness, had a side effect which my daughter

130

found intolerable: it caused her to gain weight. She therefore chose to put a halt to the treatment and to accept herself as an asthmatic. She would often sleep sitting upright in an armchair to facilitate her breathing.'

'Could you describe the plaintiff's behaviour during one of these attacks?'

'There's nothing to describe. She seemed to be labouring under the weight of an enormous burden. It was as though she had an accordian in place of her lungs. Grating, sighing notes of music, impossible chords, would emerge from her throat.'

'And these attacks usually occurred when the plaintiff was over-excited?'

'Yes.'

'Thus, when she claims to have heard panting and gasping during the events whose exact nature we are here to establish, it is not unfeasible that these noises might have originated in her own body?'

. . .

'Please note that I'm not saying this *was* the case, Madam, I'm simply asking whether such a hypothesis belongs to the realm of possibility or not. Allow me to remind you that you are under oath.'

'I can't answer that question. At the time of the events, I hadn't seen my daughter for several months. I know nothing of her state of mind and body during that period.'

'And yet you know that she had just filled out a declaration for loss of keys, and that she had voluntarily locked herself up in the Castle. Do these acts not suggest, at the very least, a predisposition to the over-excited state which was apt to bring on panting and gasping? . . . I understand quite well, Madam, that your maternal sentiment might urge you to protect the plaintiff, but it should not lead you to deny the obvious.'

So the Owl and I both started running through the forest, forgetting all about looking for paths and listening for roads, we ran at random, in every direction, in mad zig-zags. The Owl ran faster than I did, it was only natural, I kept tripping up on roots, plunging forward onto sharp stones, scrambling through bushes, whereas he – at the very most, he may have got his face slapped by a few branches . . . And then, I get to my feet after a fall: and he is gone. Silence . . . Within the silence, Omaya's heart is hammering. Behind her, to the left and to the right, the forest beasts are breathing. Panting hoarsely, avidly, savagely. Omaya hurtles forward, falls again, gets up, the panting follows her in a crescendo . . . and suddenly, she finds herself at the edge of the road. Beep, beep! She spins around, her eyes popping out of their sockets.

'Good heavens, it's a young girl! What on earth are you doing out in the middle of the forest in the middle of the night?'

'I'm looking for my father, we were out walking and I fell down, I'm lost.'

'Get in, get in, we'll go and look for your daddy together. It's cold out.'

'No, thanks just the same, I'll wait for him here, he's sure to show up.'

'But you can't just stand there all alone at the edge of the road, it's dangerous! Good thing I saw you, the forest is full of weirdos at this time of night. Come on, get in, you run more of a risk out there than in here, I assure you.'

Run. Omaya plunges back into the forest, and the car thunders away. Little by little, her heart calms down. The trees breathe more peacefully. The wind passes through their bronchi without a sound. And at last, after a long while, Omaya remembers the song of the Owl. She calls out softly: *Whoo! Whoo!* And to her right, a mere few steps away, the Owl answers: *Whoo! Whoo!*

'This is absurd. We cannot accept *whoo-whoos* as evidence.'

'That's not what I intended them to be, your Honour.'

'Your speech is getting more ludicrous by the second. This constant recourse to metaphors and onomatopoeia is inadmissible. What we need are *facts*.'

'I quite agree, your Honour.'

'And the facts, such as we've been able to reconstruct them up to now, are in flagrant contradiction to all this bucolic poppy-cock. Among other things, it has been established that the plaintiff is a woman of the city, not to say a woman of the streets. She's never set foot in the country, and in all probability knows nothing about nature. So what are these recurring images of forests and of lakes? *Where* did she used to go walking at night with her father? And of what relevance to the case are all these stars, branches and roots, to say nothing of the inimitable thorn in her heel? This cannot go on any longer; we need to know where things stand. *What*, exactly, is the plaintiff's father going round? *What* private property did he trespass on? And *what*, in heaven's name, is the meaning of the vacant eyes you've been harping on about since the very beginning?'

'Given the fact that these are very painful memories, and that, moreover, they have no direct bearing upon the December incident, I judged it advisable to respect my client's privacy by presenting them to you in a somewhat . . . attenuated form.'

'I'm the Judge here – not you; I alone decide on the relevance or irrelevance of each and every element in the file. I'm warning you for the last time: inundating us with fiction can only harm your client's case.'

Poor Anastasia.

'In your opinion, Counsel for the Prosecution, would it be advisable to question this woman's father?'

'Advisable perhaps, but impossible unfortunately. He, too has lost his keys and been incapable of good conduct for the past several years.'

'Genetic antecedents, then?'

'Indeed. What a patrimony.'

'And mightn't there be some other man, someone close to the plaintiff, who might have taken, so to speak, her father's place?'

'There is Saroyan, so-called.'

'Summon Saroyan, so-called, to the witness stand.'

'Do you swear to tell the truth, the whole truth and nothing but the truth? Raise your right hand; say: I swear.'

'I don't claim to know the whole truth.'

'Might your testimony be incriminating for the plaintiff?'

'Yes.'

'That is sufficient. State your family name, your Christian name, your age and your profession.'

'Saroyan. Full stop. That is all.'

'What is your relationship to the plaintiff?'

'Surrogate father.'

'Please describe your role in the parthenogenesis of her malady.'

'I used to buy her flowers.'

'Flowers?'

'Yes. That was the name she gave to her various medicines.'

'Ah . . . And what sort of . . . flower did she have a predilection for?'

'That is a professional secret. I can, however, tell you that when we were working on the Plague, the plaintiff had absorbed a staggering quantity of anti-asthmatic pills. Her body had swollen so as to be almost unrecognisable.'

'Were you the one who procured her the pills in question?'

'No. The plaintiff had her prescription for them renewed regularly by her doctor, without, meanwhile, having consumed the ones she'd bought before. She'd accumulated a very impressive stock.'

'Had you seen this stock?'

'With my own eyes. For the plaintiff, this particular drug did not count as a flower. She thought of it as bread. Her doctor was a god, and she used to pray to him: Give us this day our daily bread.'

Alix would tell me constantly: Get up, defend yourself, you have legs to run and kick with, not to kneel and pray. Stop begging their assistance, their forgiveness, every time you feel like taking anything on.

When Alix got down on her knees, it was to prove her independence once again. To change the flat tyre all by herself. Omaya standing at the edge of the road, watching her. Empty-handed, empty-headed. Nightfall, rainfall. How does she know about all these things, why didn't the Owl ever show me, the bolts, the wedge, the arm's strength increased tenfold by the tools? Alix manipulates the jack with consummate ease. Metal scraping against metal . . . and beyond that, intermittently, the hissing of tyres on wet pavement. Omaya stands in front of the car, in the beam of the headlights. I'm so cold, I'm freezing cold . . .

135

'Couldn't you at least give me a hand?'

'My hands are freezing. I'm trying to warm them up in the headlights.'

'Those lights are cold, Omaya. You'll get warm a lot faster if you move around a bit. Come and help me.'

The sound of brakes. A car has passed us, its brakes have screeched on and now it's backing up towards us, it's a police car. Two men in uniform get out and walk towards Omaya.

'Trouble?'

'A flat tyre. My friend was just saying that she needed a hand.'

Alix says: What's going on? She raises her head. In the uncertain light I can see her red cheeks turning white.

'What do you want?'

'Got a puncture, have you? Got a spare tyre?'

'We've got everything we need. We don't need you on top of it.'

'Your friend back there said you did.'

'Well, if she needs you, go and discuss it with her.'

'Hang on! That's no way to speak to an officer of the law. Is this your car?'

'Yeah, it is. Is that yours?'

'Let me see your insurance – and your driving licence, while you're at it.'

'Let me see your ass.'

She didn't say that. But she could have said it. She was trembling with rage. And afterwards:

'It's your fault. They only stopped because they'd seen you strutting about in front of the headlights. Can't you survive without a stage for five minutes? Do you have to be under a spotlight every second of your life? Like a whore at her lamp post?'

The whore, the fallen woman. How does one go about hitching lifts? You stand at the edge of the road and wait for someone to pick you up . . . Within a second they've sized you up and come to a decision: Okay, get in . . . or else they've decided against you. You stand there waiting, the cars pass you by, the eyes look you over and turn away: they don't want you. You don't have the right to get in any more. Your charms have deteriorated, you're no longer a young girl. At best, they'll pick you up out of pity, they'll say to you condescendingly: Go ahead, get in. They'll express surprise that, at your age, you still haven't got your own means of transport. They'll look you over suspiciously, wondering whether you're still worth picking up.

Do not give the slightest credence to the popular misconception according to which this can only happen to pretty young girls. Don't think you're out of danger just because you're on the far side of twenty. Between the ages of six months and ninety-six years, you are a potential target. It might be useful, however, if you absolutely have to go out alone, to imitate the walk – not of an elderly lady, since old age is synonymous with vulnerability – but of a matron. That's it: walk like the tired mother of a large family, with heavy yet rather hurried steps. Not too hurried, though – if you start to run, they'll know for sure you're not inviolable.

During the Plague tour, Saroyan would pass me the wheel from time to time. As though it went without saying. As though he hadn't noticed that nothing went without saying any more. I'd invariably get wedged behind an enormous truck.

'Go ahead and pass him, what are you waiting for?'

We're on a two-lane road and it never seems to be the right time to pass. Going uphill we slow down until we've almost stopped, asphyxiated by the black fumes, going downhill the lorry speeds up, and even on flat stretches how can I be certain, if I pull out to the left, how can I know for sure that another lorry won't suddenly loom up ahead, I wouldn't have seen it because of a slight curve or an invisible bump in the road, and all at once it would be there, and I wouldn't be able to let go of the steering-wheel and put my hands over my eyes, I'm not sitting between the Owl's knees any more . . .

Saroyan is getting nervous. He says we're falling behind, the other actors will arrive hours before we do, so Omaya puts on the left indicator and moves over into the left-hand lane, she steps on the accelerator with all her might, glides up next to the lorry but can't pull out in front of it, suddenly she sees headlights up ahead, a car is approaching, unthinkably fast, she slams on the brakes and Saroyan cries out: What the hell are you doing? Another car has already taken her place behind the lorry, she puts on the right indicator and brakes again, the other car slows down and lets her re-enter the right-hand lane, at that very instant the approaching car roars past with an indignant honk of its horn. Saroyan's hand is clutching the door handle. He remains silent. The car behind theirs pulls out and passes them, tooting in its turn. Omaya remains silent, too, for fear that a scarlet droplet might fall from her mouth: her teeth have cut through her upper lip.

'I thought you said Saroyan didn't have a car.'

Then let's say I'm driving Cybele's car, I'm wedged behind a lorry, he puts on his left indicator but doesn't move, I conclude he's telling me I can pass him so I put on my own left indicator and pull out into the left-hand lane, just at that moment the lorry makes a left turn and I smash into him, I kill the driver and am crippled for life.

Or else: the car behind me is flashing its headlights at me, teasing me, sitting on my tail, I accelerate without noticing that another car is coming down the link road from the right, chock full of luggage and children, we collide at top speed . . . Pile-up! Final total: three dead and six wounded.

Or again: I'm on a three-lane road, and just when I pull out into the middle lane to pass a lorry, a car coming in the opposite direction does the same. Head-on collision; final total: two dead, myself and the other driver.

'But in actual fact, you've never had an accident, have you?'

'What do you mean . . . in actual fact?'

'In fact, in reality, none of this has ever happened. You're here, you're alive; you've never had any dealings with insurance companies, have you? You've never been the cause of anybody's death. Neither Saroyan's, nor the children's, nor your own.'

In actual fact I'm here, I'm alive. None of this ever happened. In actual fact, that evening, I didn't even leave the Castle. I spent the whole night dreaming and in the morning I went and told my dreams to the police and to the doctors and to the lawyers and to her Honour. No one has committed a crime, not even a misdemeanour: the proof is that I'm not dead.

'You don't want to settle for assault and battery?'
'No.'
'You're sure you want to contest the decision?'

139

'Yes.'

'You have the strength?'

'At the moment, no . . . But that isn't the point.'

'I understand how much it means to you, Omaya, and of course I'll continue to defend you. But we failed the first time round, I can't promise you the outcome will be different the second time. I must admit I'm not too optimistic.'

'Anastasia, if we leave it at that, I'll never be strong again.'

'So we appeal?'

'Yes.'

We appeal to you. We beg you to hear us. We get down on our knees.

'Let's see – turn her this way a bit? Not bad. Try and make her kneel down.'

'She's not very cooperative . . . Dammit!'

'You start kicking, love, you're gonna get kicked right in the belly – and it won't be with bare feet, either. Make her kneel down.'

'She's pretty bloody stubborn . . . Do as you're told, will you?'

'Don't slap her in the face – it'll show.'

'The chest, then.'

'The chest, that's it. With the flat of your hand.'

'She still doesn't want to kneel down. What a sack of bones! I bet she's going to start throwing up again.'

They said that. I beg you to believe me. Even if I had a hard time remembering their faces, even if I've had nightmares now and then and occasionally heightened my own plots, I can tell the difference between reality and the rest, this is reality, I swear it, their words, their gestures, I could never be wrong about that, they'll never go away, they're like a needle coming back over and over again to the same groove in the record, to the same vein in the arm, like a pin thrust into the brain, at the same spot every time, the same words keep coming back over and over and I can't escape them . . .

'Your story still isn't clear.'

'CLARITY IS SYNONYMOUS WITH BEAUTY!'

'Calm down. Try to remember. Let yourself go.'

'. . . Okay . . . I had to go to the station. That much I remember. My train was due to leave at exactly ten o'clock.'

'Ten in the morning or ten in the evening?'

'Ten in the morning.'

'Just like your appointment with me?'

. . .

'Go on.'

'But in order to get to the station, I had to take the underground . . . I bought a newspaper before entering the bowels of the earth, and once underway I got absorbed in an article I was reading . . .'

'What was the article about?'

'I can't remember . . . No, I really can't remember.'

'When you say remember, do you perhaps mean the opposite of dismember? You have a hard time remembering yourself?'

. . .

'All right. What happened next? You were so absorbed in reading the article that . . .'

'That I went right past the station where I was supposed to get off. And when I came out of the underground I had no idea where I was, it was a terrifying neighbourhood

141

whose existence I'd never even suspected . . .'

'Why did you go back above ground, rather than taking the underground in the opposite direction?'

'A . . . a moment's distraction . . .'

'And this neighbourhood – what did it look like?'

'It was a world of glass and metal, the building structures seemed at the same time geometrical and organic, so hideous that they turned my blood to ice . . . There were shops everywhere, with flashy, dazzling display-windows, and in the windows . . . Alix was with me, I don't know how we'd met up, but at this point we were walking along together . . .'

'Yes? And in the windows?'

'. . . Hundreds of naked dummies. Standing, sitting, kneeling, lying down, women's bodies frozen in every conceivable position, disarticulated dolls . . . But I started walking faster and faster, I could see the station clock in the distance, it was ten minutes to ten and I still hadn't bought my ticket . . .'

'Indeed . . . And then?'

'. . . And then, all of a sudden, Alix started pulling at my arm and saying: Look! Look! . . . In one of the shop-windows, frozen and naked amidst the dummies, there was a live woman. Her eyes implored us. Alix said we should storm into the store right then and there, make a scene, set the captive free, but I didn't have time, I absolutely had to catch my train, that was the only thing in the world that mattered . . .'

'And yet this woman was suffering a kind of torment you knew quite well – one with which you'd been familiar, so to speak, since the day you were born. Isn't that right?'

'I don't understand.'

'The glass box? . . . But then, you had a train to catch.'

'Yes . . . I shook my arm free of Alix's grip, I saw her

142

eyes go dark with shock and hatred, the prisoner's eyes go dark with despair . . . And then, I'm on the station platform . . . and I see the train pulling out. It's too late. I've failed at everything. There's nothing left.'

'I must request you not to light that cigarette. You know the rule: no crutches in this room. Cigarettes are crutches, you lean on them for support.'

It's not that, it's just so there'll be a smokescreen between Omaya and the enemy, in the coffee-shop it didn't work, I lit up a cigarette and they saw me just the same, whereas I was unable to look at them, incapable of describing their physical appearance. Smoking is forbidden in the court-room, too, they won't allow me to protect myself in any way, they just keep telling me I have nothing to fear within the confines of the court . . .

'This time, when the defendants are led into the dock, you mustn't hide your face in your hands.'

'I can't see them, I've already told you that, I simply can't.'

'Omaya, Justice demands that we look reality in the face. Justice herself is blind, she wears a blindfold over her eyes, but from everyone else she requires clear-sighted-ness, lucidity.'

'That isn't true, Justice is like me, both of us hide our eyes so as not to see, that's exactly what happened last time, she refused to remove her blindfold, she didn't see a thing, and she declared: Assault and battery.'

'You mustn't talk that way – it's dangerous.'

'You know perfectly well that smoking is dangerous. Especially for someone like you, who's had serious disorders of the respiratory tract, smoking is playing with

143

fire, you're polluting your body, the haven of your mind, listen to me, Omaya, all you get is one body, it has to last your whole life long, the damage you inflict on it is permanent, every puff you take poisons you a bit more, every packet you smoke shortens your life by several hours.'

'The world is full of poisons, Cybele, everything's infected, absolutely everything, I think of cigarettes as a sort of vaccination, I knowingly absorb small doses of their venom so as to develop an immunity – that is the principle of inoculation, isn't it?'

'But that's not at all what you should want! To develop an immunity, to become impermeable, indifferent to the problems of the world! What characterises man is precisely his capacity to *act* upon these problems, be sensitive to them, and use his intelligence in the service of his sensitivity. The numbing of the senses can bring about an atrophy of sense itself, of meaning . . . Why are you looking at me that way? You frighten me . . .'

'I'm a woman now, Cybele. You're no longer required to keep me alive. You're going to have to renounce your motherly duty.'

'But I love you, darling, it's not a question of duty, how can I help but suffer when I see you going up in smoke?'

'Give us the exact meaning of the saying: There's no smoke without fire. Your answer will be timed as per usual.'

'I can't go on.'

'Hurry up, hurry up, the stop-watch is already ticking.'

'No! I'm the one who gives these orders, so I can refuse to obey them, too.'

'No way, no way, you may not disobey, I am pedagogically responsible for you. When you failed at University, you chose to become an autodidact, well, I'm your auto . . .'

'Oh, no!'

'Oh, yes, I am, I'm your auto, and as such I have the right to didact you, your time is running out, your score will be shameful, come on, come on, give us the meaning . . .'

'But I'm the one who's thinking all of this, and I'm the one who's thinking but I'm the one who's thinking all of this, and I'm the one who's thinking I'm the one who's thinking but I'm the one who's thinking all of this, and . . .'

'You're heading straight for disaster. None shall be saved but by me. There's no smoke without fire: there – grab onto that – you see? I rescued you from disaster, now you'll have to answer.'

'. . . There's no smoke without fire, that means that when you light up a cigarette, you think you can protect yourself behind the smokescreen, whereas, in fact, it isn't a means of protection but a means of destruction, the inner fires are gradually consuming the bronchi of the trees, you're committing intimate arson, the alveoli are reduced to ashes, you can't breathe, everyone knows that in fires one doesn't die of burns but of asphyxiation, you dance until you're breathless and in the end you go up in flames, and all that's left of your identity is a charred ballet shoe.'

'Your answers are growing more and more inappropriate. Try to get hold of yourself. Let's do some arithmetic: how many cigarettes have you smoked in your life? Assuming that every year for the past twenty years you've smoked one more cigarette per day than the year before – how many would that make?'

'I have no idea.'

'It's very simple. You started smoking twenty years ago, at the rate of one cigarette per day. The first year you therefore smoked 365 cigarettes; let this amount be n. Thereafter, year 2 will be $n + 365$ or $2(365)$, year 3 will be $3(365)$, and so forth, so that to obtain the correct answer all you have to do is add $20(365) + 19(365) + 18(365)\ldots + n$. Well?'

'That makes a lot of cigarettes.'

'I didn't ask you to share your intuitive appreciation with me, but to provide me with a precise and incontrovertible response supported by mathematical proof.'

'They need proof, Omaya. Ever since they found out about the drugs you used for your role as the baker, they've grown suspicious. They think you capable of anything, including having made up the whole story to justify your lack of keys.'

'Why did you leave the Castle?'

'Sorry? Oh, please, I'm sorry, please forgive me, I didn't hear you, the Friends are singing and I can't hear myself think.'

'Why did you enter the Castle? What had gone wrong on that particular day?'

The Friends continue to sing. The policemen caress their truncheons with increasing frenzy.

'Objection, Your Honour. It seems to me the court has already spent enough time reviewing my client's past history.'

The gavel falls. The truncheons grow erect.

'Silence in the court! If there is any further disturbance, the remainder of the trial will be held *in camera*. Now, please answer the question put to you by the Prosecutor.'

'The Prosecutor?'

'Yes.'

'But she's a woman . . .'

'We don't say: the Prosecutress, for obvious phonetic reasons. Stop beating about the bush, this nonsense has lasted long enough.'

'. . . Well, that day, I'd left the Flat with the intention of going to the Theatre, the Flat was never a Theatre any more, my clothes were rotting in the cupboard and so was the food in the fridge . . .'

'Please try to express yourself more clearly, and to give us nothing but the relevant details. Allow me to draw your attention to the fact that, by your lawyer's own admission, you were no longer living in your flat at this time, and your theatre company had disbanded. Kindly stick to the version of the facts that has already been set down by the clerk.'

'I beg your pardon . . . As I was leaving the Flat, I must have had a moment's distraction . . . I slammed the door . . .'

'I see. And then what?'

'I noticed that my keys were still inside. I hammered madly on the door, but no one came to open it. So I went to the Castle and filled out a declaration for loss of keys.'

'And yet your keys can hardly be said to have been lost. You knew quite well where they were.'

'Yes, but they were inaccessible to me. It was as though they didn't exist.'

'I will allow the members of the jury to draw their own conclusions from the confession the plaintiff has just made. When things exist, she is capable of acting as though they don't; it follows logically than when things do not exist, she is capable of acting as though they do. No further questions, your Honour.'

'OMAYA!'

'. . . Yes?'

'I asked you a question.'

'I'm sorry, I didn't hear you, I must have dozed off for a second, could you repeat the question? Please repeat it, I promise I'll do my best to find the answer.'

'It was the most important question of all, Omaya. The question which – precisely because it was so important – can never be repeated. If you didn't hear it the first time, there's nothing more we can do for you. It's no longer possible to save you, it's all over, we're very sorry, we've done everything in our power, you'll get only what you deserve: a nought. That is the final verdict. You have only yourself to blame. The evidence is overwhelming: this time, you may not appeal.'

'I – what? I can't appeal?'

'Out of the question. We gave you your chance, we tried to make things easy for you, we took all the necessary precautions, we humoured you, we nursed you, we coddled you, and you never showed the slightest sign of gratitude, all you did was complain and keep on complaining, so there you are, the verdict has been given: it's a nought, and it serves you right. Full stop. That is all.'

'But we can't possibly stop there, it's unthinkable, a nought won't allow itself to be thought, it's the very absence of all thought, we can't leave it at that, how do you expect me to live with a nought in my body, with a gaping hole in my memory, how do you expect me to walk down the street, look people in the eye . . .? You're trying to annihilate me all over again, but I won't acknowledge defeat, you say I deserve a nought, that's what *they've* always said, you're in cahoots, you reached this verdict together ahead of time, it's a mockery of Justice, I'll tear the blindfold away from Justice's eyes and she'll see clearly at long last, she'll burst out laughing, she'll come down from her pedestal with her arms outstretched to embrace me, she'll join in the circle of Friends, so beautiful, so beautiful, mothers will be reunited with their daughters, all of us will dance together and the whole courtroom will start to spin, I swear it!'

'You have nothing left to swear. You're excluded from the court. A police car is waiting outside to take you back to the Castle.'

'No!'

'In a strait-jacket, if need be. The court is adjourned.'

'But we haven't even heard the defendants!'

'The car is waiting. Please be silent. The incident is closed. Evacuate the courtroom.'

The gavel falls. It's the beginning of the play. It's the end of the world.

'NO!'

'No one can hear your screams. The room is deserted. It's too late.'

'But we haven't even heard the defendants!'

Of course: Omaya's the one who can't hear them. How could I have heard them when they were trampling me underfoot? But you – you've never heard anyone but them. Driving along in their literary vehicles – so lyrical, so cathartic – they would point out to you the beauties of the countryside . . . by car, fast and far . . . and little did it matter to you who was getting crushed beneath the wheels. Each of them at the wheel, taking turns . . . turning roles . . . rolling past . . . extolling past . . . NO! It's not over yet, it can't end this way, nothing's been decided yet, it's up to you to take the decision . . . to take the wheel . . . your turn to play . . . your play to turn . . . your wheel to roll . . . your role to play . . . NO! That isn't what I mean, it's the words that talk that way, the words have contracted a serious illness, they've been infected by the plague, they're buboes swelling in my brain, pustules bursting under pressure, and yet the rose was such a lovely, shocking pink, pink with a violet heart . . . NO! . . . Bang! Right in the heart . . . right on target . . . rifle discharge . . . electrical discharge . . . They fasten the electrodes to your temples and then discharge, the electricity engraves on you its spasms, its orgasms, it ravages your body and soul and leaves you for dead . . . They fasten their hands on your hips and then discharge . . . lightning bolt . . . the electricity whips through your entrails, trounces your heart and leaves you for dead . . . An actress climbs into her bathtub filled with cold water, she stands there fully dressed, unscrews the ceiling lightbulb, wets her fingers and plunges them into the socket . . . Conflagration! Electrocution! Successful suicide . . . No, no one has died like that so far . . . All the more reason for Omaya to do so . . . to be condemned to the electric chair . . . get it over with once and for all . . . They bind her wrists and ankles with straps hooked up to the city current, they slip an electrode helmet over her head and then discharge . . . STOP IT! Bull's eye . . . the eye of the cyclone . . . cyclamen makes the sweetest fruits and flowers . . . strange and strangling . . . dusky peace makes the sweetest years and hours . . . strong and dangling . . . soapy rain makes the sweetest baths and showers . . . string and wrangling . . . aftermath makes the sweetest boughs and bowers . . . straight and narrow . . . off the path . . . destination . . . desinence . . . resonance . . . words without rhyme or reason . . . Before long they won't even be words any more, nothing but a mush of syllables, and you'll have to clamp down the lid or else the alphabet soup will boil over . . . Let's talk it over . . . Let's talk openly . . . OPEN

THROAT SHALL BE LAW ... I've opened my heart to you
... open-heart operation ... VIOLATED HEART DARES TO
KILL ... I'd never dare ... That's not what I'm asking for
... all I'm asking for is justice ... blindfolded Justice ...
assault and battery ... NO! Don't say that! ROSE WITH
VIOLET HEART ... the rose mattered ... shivered and
shattered ... assaulted and battered ... NO! Don't say
that, don't say that, it's not true, I was knocked off at
point blank range ...

'EVERYBODY OFF.'